생활 속의 참선수행 Practice in Daily Life ⑥

온 우주를 살리는 마음의 불씨

The Spark That Can Save The Universe

온 우주를 살리는 마음의 불씨
대행큰스님 법문
생활 속의 참선수행 ⑥ / 한영합본

발행일	2010년 10월 초판
	2014년 1월 2판1쇄
영문번역	한마음국제문화원
표지디자인	박수연
편집	한마음국제문화원
발행	한마음출판사
출판등록	384-2000-000010
전화	031-470-3175
팩스	031-471-6928
이메일	onemind@hanmaum.org

© 2014 (재)한마음선원
본 출판물은 저작권법에 의하여 보호를 받는 저작물이므로 무단 복제와 무단 전재를 할 수 없습니다.

The Spark That Can Save The Universe
Dharma Talks by Seon Master Daehaeng
Practice in Daily Life ⑥
Bilingual Korean/English

First Edition Printed Oct. 2010
Second Edition Printed Jan. 2014
English Translation by
Hanmaum International Culture Institute
Edited by Hanmaum International Culture Institute
Cover Design by Su Yeon Park
Published by Hanmaum Publications

© 2014 Hanmaum Seonwon Foundation
All rights reserved, including the right to reproduce this work in any form.

Printed in Republic of Korea

ISBN 978-89-91857-29-2 (04220)/**978-89-951830-0-7(set)**

국립중앙도서관 출판시도서목록(CIP)

온 우주를 살리는 마음의 불씨 = (The) spark that can save the universe : 대행 큰스님 법문: 한영합본 / 영문번역: 한마음국제문화원. -- [안양] : 한마음출판사, 2014
　p. ;　　cm. — (생활 속의 참선수행 = Practice in daily life ; 6)

한영 대역본임
ISBN 978-89-9857-29-2 04220 : ₩6000
ISBN 89-951830-0-4(세트) 04220

법문(불경)[法文]
225.2-KDC5
294.34-DDC21　　　　　　CIP2013028521

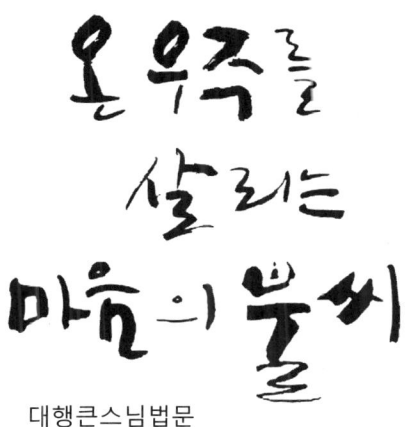

대행큰스님법문

The Spark That Can Save The Universe

Dharma Talks by
Seon Master Daehaeng

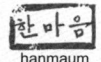

내 한생각이 법이 되어

한철 살림 하면서
마음 닦아 깨달으면
내 한생각 법이 되어
내 나라 살리고,
온누리에 얼음 녹아
만골짜기 흘러흘러
고기떼 춤을 추고,
꽃피고 새 울어
스스로 열매 익어
만가지 맛 알게 되리.

찰나 생활 하면서
마음 닦아 깨달으면
내 한생각 지혜 되어
지구촌 살리고,
온누리에 천차만별
생명들이 눈을 뜨고,
마음의 바다 위에
여여히 밝아서
스스로 빛이 되어
본래 자리 눈뜨리니.

- 대행큰스님 게송 -

As Your One Thought Becomes Dharma

While living for this brief season,
if you cultivate your mind and awaken,
your one thought manifests in the world
and saves the world.
The ice melts,
sending water flowing into ten thousand valleys.
The fish dance and play,
flowers bloom and birds sing,
and the fruit ripens naturally.
May all beings know its ten thousand flavors.

In the midst of life changing in every instant,
if you cultivate your mind and awaken,
a single thought becomes wisdom
and saves this village we all live in.
Across the world innumerable beings open their eyes,
each shining like the moon over the sea of mind,
each becoming bright,
their eyes opening
to their inherent foundation.

– Daehaeng Kun Sunim –

차 례

10　머리글

14　대행큰스님에 대하여

22　온 우주를 살리는 마음의 불씨

Contents

11 Foreword

15 About Daehaeng Kun Sunim

23 The Spark That Can Save The Universe

머리글

대행큰스님께서 지난 50여 년 동안 끊임없이 중생들에게 베풀어주신 수많은 법문이 있었지만, 핵심을 짚어내는 단 하나의 단어가 있다면, 그건 아마도 "참나"일 것입니다. 항상 나와 함께 있어서 보지 못하는 내 안의 진짜 나, 그 "참나"를 발견하여 당당하고 싱그럽게 살아가기를 바라는, 중생을 위한 스님의 간절한 바램은 이 한 편의 법문 속에도 여지없이 드러나 있습니다.

누구에게나 내면에는 만물만생을 다 먹여 살리고도 되남는 마음 속 한 점의 불씨가 있습니다. 그 영원한 불씨를 찾아 광대무변한 마음법의 이치를 체득하여, 진정한 자유인으로서, 우주의 한 일원으로서 당당히 그 역할을 해나가길 바라는 대행큰스님의 간곡한 뜻이 이 법문을 통해 여러분 모두의 마음에 전해지길 바랍니다.

한마음국제문화원 일동 합장

Foreword

Over the last fifty years, Daehaeng Kun Sunim has given countless Dharma talks and teachings to beings without number, but if all those talks could be summed up into one word, it would be "true self."

This true essence has always been with us, yet remains unseen. Discover it for yourself, and in doing so, learn to live with courage, dignity, and joy. That all beings should awaken to this true essence is Daehaeng Kun Sunim's deepest wish. When you've tasted the purest, most refreshing spring water imaginable, you naturally want to share it with others.

Within us all is this seed, this spark that feeds and sustains each and every being. Discover this eternal spark and realize its profound and unlimited ability. If you can do this, you'll know what it means to truly be a free person, and you can fulfill the great role that is yours as a member of the whole universe.

With palms together,
the Hanmaum International Culture Institute

끊임없이

지혜로운 길로

인도하는

대자비의 어머니

나의 주인공,

진정한 나의 스승에게

*To our true teacher,
selfless, compassionate
the mother of all,
endlessly guiding us
from within
and without.*

대행큰스님에 대하여

대행큰스님은 여러 면에서 매우 보기 드문 선사(禪師)셨다. 무엇보다 선사라면 당연히 비구스님을 떠올리는 전통 속에서 여성으로서 선사가 되었으며, 비구스님들을 제자로 두었던 유일한 비구니 스님이었고, 노년층 여성이 주된 신도계층을 이루었던 한국 불교에 젊은 세대의 청장년층 남녀들을 대거 참여하게 만들어 한국불교에 새로운 풍격(風格)을 일으키는데 일조한 큰 스승이셨다. 또한 어느 누구나 마음수행을 통해 깨달을 수 있음을 강조하며 전통적인 수행 모델과는 달리 삭발제자와 유발제자를 가리지 않고 법을 구하는 이들에게는 모두 똑같이 가르침을 주셨고, 전통 비구니 강원과 비구니 종단에 대한 지속적인 지원을 펼치심으로써 비구니승단을 발전시키는데 중추적인 역할을 하셨다.

About Daehaeng Kun Sunim

Daehaeng *Kun Sunim*[1] (1927-2012) was a rare teacher in Korea: a female *Seon(Zen)*[2] master, a nun whose students included monks as well as nuns, and a teacher who helped revitalize Korean Buddhism by dramatically increasing the participation of young people and men. She broke out of traditional models of spiritual practice to teach in such a way that allowed anyone to practice and awaken, making laypeople a particular focus of her efforts. At the same time, she was a major force for the advancement of *Bhikkunis*,[3] heavily supporting traditional nuns' colleges as well as the modern Bhikkuni Council of Korea.

1. Sunim / Kun Sunim: Sunim is the respectful title of address for a Buddhist monk or nun in Korea, and Kun Sunim s the title given to outstanding nuns or monks.

2. Seon (Chan, Zen): Seon describes the unshakeable state where one has firm faith in their inherent foundation, their Buddha-nature, and so returns everything they encounter back to this fundamental mind. It also means letting go of "I," "me," and "mine" throughout one's daily life.

3. Bhikkunis: Female sunims who are fully ordained are called Bhikkuni(比丘尼), while male sunims who are fully ordained are called Bhikku(比丘). This can also be a polite way of indicating male or female sunims.

대행스님은 1927년 서울에서 태어나 일찍이 9세경에 자성을 밝히시고, 일제 강점기와 6.25 전쟁을 거치면서 당신이 증득(證得)하신 바를 완성하기 위해 오랫동안 산중에서 수행하셨다. 1950년대 말경, 치악산 상원사 근처에 있는 한 움막에 머무르시며 찾아오는 수많은 사람들의 고통스런 호소를 들으시고 그들을 도와주셨다. 중생들이 가지고 오는 어떠한 문제도, 어떠한 어려운 상황도 해결이 되도록 도와주신 대행스님의 자비의 원력은 당시에 이미 한국에서는 전설이 되어 있었다. 스님은 자비를 물 마른 웅덩이에서 죽어가는 물고기를 살리는 방생에 비유하셨다. 그래서 집세가 없어 셋집에서 쫓겨난 사람들에게 집을 마련해 주고, 학비가 없어서 학교를 마칠 수 없는 학생들에게 학비를 대주셨지만, 스님의 자비행(慈悲行)을 아는 사람은 거의 없을 정도였다.

Born in Seoul, Korea, she awakened when she was around eight years old and spent the years that followed learning to put her understanding into practice. For years, she wandered the mountains of Korea, wearing ragged clothes and eating only what was at hand. Later, she explained that she hadn't been pursuing some type of asceticism; rather, she was just completely absorbed in entrusting everything to her fundamental *Buddha*[4] essence and observing how that affected her life.

Those years profoundly shaped Kun Sunim's later teaching style; she intimately knew the great potential, energy, and wisdom inherent within each of us, and recognized that most of the people she encountered suffered because they didn't realize this about themselves. Seeing clearly the great light in every individual, she taught people to rely upon this inherent foundation, and refused to teach anything that distracted from this most important truth.

---

4. Buddha: In this text, "Buddha" and "Bodhisattva" are capitalized out of respect, because these represent the essence and function of the enlightened mind. "The Buddha" always refers to Shakyamuni Buddha.

그러나, 문제를 해결해 주면 그때뿐 또 다른 문제가 닥쳐오면 속수무책이 되어 버리고 마는 사람들을 보며, 스님께서는 중생들이 자신들의 문제를 스스로 해결하고, 나아가 인과(因果)와 윤회(輪廻)¹의 굴레에서 벗어나 자유인이 될 수 있는 도리를 가르치는 것이 더 시급하다는 생각을 하게 되셨다.

마침내 산에서 내려온 스님께서는 1972년 경기도 안양에 한마음선원을 설립하셨고, 이후 40여 년 동안 한마음선원에 주석하시며, 크고 작은 법회에서 질문을 해오는 사람들에게 그들의 근기와 여건에 맞추어 답을 해주시며 불법의 진리를 가르쳐 주셨다. 스님은 여러 다양한 사회복지 프로그램을 후원하셨고, 6개국에 10개의 해외지원과 한국 국내에 15개 지원을 세우셨으며, 스님의 가르침은 영어, 독어, 스페인어, 러시아어, 중국어, 일본어, 불어, 이태리어, 베트남어, 인도네시아어, 아랍어 등으로 번역 출간되었다. 2012년 5월 21일 자정, 향년 86세로 입적하셨으며, 법랍 63세셨다.

---

1. 윤회(輪廻): 산스크리트의 삼사라(samsara)를 번역한 말로 쉼 없이 돈다는 생사의 바퀴를 뜻함. 다시 말해, 수레바퀴가 끊임없이 구르는 것과 같이, 중생이 번뇌와 업에 의하여 삼계(三界: 색계, 욕계, 무색계) 육도(六道: 지옥, 아귀, 축생, 아수라, 인간, 천상)라는 생사의 세계를 그치지 않고 돌고 도는 현상을 일컬음.

Her deep compassion made her a legend in Korea long before she formally started teaching. She was known for having the spiritual power to help people in all circumstances with every kind of problem. She compared compassion to freeing a fish from a drying puddle, putting a homeless family into a home, or providing the school fees that would allow a student to finish high school. And when she did things like this, and much more, few knew that she was behind it.

Kun Sunim saw that for people to live freely and go forward in the world as a blessing to all around them, they needed to know about this bright essence that is within each of us. To help people discover this for themselves, she founded the first *Hanmaum*[5] Seon Center in 1972. For the next forty years she gave wisdom to those who needed wisdom, food and money to those who were poor and hungry, and compassion to those who were hurting.

---

5. Hanmaum[han-ma-um]: "Han" means one, great, and combined, while "maum" means mind, as well as heart, and together they mean everything combined and connected as one. What is called "Hanmaum" is intangible, unseen, and transcends time and space. It has no beginning or end, and is sometimes called our fundamental mind. It also means the mind of all beings and everything in the universe connected and working together as one. In English, we usually translate this as "one mind."

본 저서는 대행큰스님의 법문을
한국어와 영어 합본 시리즈로 출간하는
<생활 속의 참선 수행>시리즈 제6권으로써
1995년 12월 17일 정기 법회 때 설하신 내용을
재편집한 것입니다.

This Dharma talk was given by
Daehaeng Kun Sunim on Sunday, December 17, 1995.
This is Volume 6 in the ongoing series,
Practice in Daily Life.
These are bilingual Korean-English editions of
individual Dharma talks by Daehaeng Kun Sunim,
with more volumes forthcoming.

Daehaeng Kun Sunim founded ten overseas branches of Hanmaum Seon Center, and her teachings have been translated into thirteen different languages to date: English, German, Russian, Chinese, French, Spanish, Indonesian, Italian, Japanese, Vietnamese, Lithuanian, Estonian, and Arabic as well as the original Korean. For more information about these or the overseas centers, please see the back of this book for details.

온 우주를 살리는 마음의 불씨

1995년 12월 17일

여러분과 한자리를 하면서도 법당 불사를 제대로 못 해, 추운 데서 동참을 하게 만들어 드려 너무나 죄송하고 몸 둘 바를 모르겠습니다. 여러분이 안 계시다면 내가 없고, 내가 없다면 여러분도 안 계시거늘, 이 한자리에 모일 때는 같이 따뜻한 데서 앉아 해야 하는데 그렇게 못 해드려서 죄송합니다. 표현하는 말만 다를 뿐, 누구나 움죽거리는 육신은 다 같고 느끼는 마음도 다 같은데 말입니다.

사정은 이렇지만 그래도 이 마음도리를 여기처럼 곧바로 들어가 공부하는 데는 별로 없는 것 같아요. 게다가 우리 한국은 불심이 돈독해서 그 선근을 이어나갈 수 있는 근기를 여러 스님네들과 더불어 많은 분들이 같이 가지고 있다고 자부합니다.

The Spark That Can Save The Universe

December 17, 1995

Even though you all came here for today's talk, many of you are sitting out in the cold because the new Dharma Hall still isn't finished. I can't tell you how bad I feel about this. Both you and I came here for the Dharma talk, so we should be able to share the same warm room. I'm so sorry not to be able to provide at least this. We all express ourselves in different ways, but this sensation of cold and discomfort is the same for each of us.

Even though the physical circumstances are somewhat difficult, there aren't many places like this, where people can learn to focus directly on their fundamental *mind*[6] and develop that potential. Further, I have no doubt that the sincere

6. Mind(心)(Kor. –maum): In Mahayana Buddhism, "mind" refers to this fundamental mind, and almost never means the brain or intellect. It is intangible, beyond space and time, and has no beginning or end. It is the source of everything, and everyone is endowed with it.

여러분이 자성삼보(自性三寶)에 귀의한다고 하시죠? 물론 여러분은 말만 들어도 자성삼보라는 그 뜻이 어디에 있다는 것을 잘 아실 겁니다. 그런데 '나의 움죽거리지 않는 근본'이라고 하면 이상스럽게 듣는 사람도 있을 겁니다. 그러나 '나의 근본'은 수레가 돌아가도 중심이 끼어진 주 중심봉 마냥 움죽거리지 않습니다. 힘만 배려해 줄 뿐이죠. 자신은 움죽거리지 않고 수레가 돌아가게 배려해 준다 이겁니다. 그와 같이 인간의 근본도 부동자세한 그 뜻으로서의 힘을 배출하고 있습니다. 그런데 근본은 힘을 배출하면서도 부동자세한 반면에, 삼라만상은 시공을 초월해서 고정됨이 없이 항상 찰나찰나 화(化) 하면서 돌아가고 있습니다.

faith and efforts of practitioners here in Korea have planted innumerable good seeds, and that the spiritual ability and strength of everyone, both sunims and laypeople, are ensuring that these roots of goodness are continuing to be planted.

Practitioners here sometimes say that they're relying upon the *Three Treasures*[7] that exist within themselves, don't they? When you hear this, you probably have a pretty good idea of what it means. However, when I refer to our inherent nature as "my unmoving foundation," this may seem like a strange expression. I describe it this way because our foundation doesn't actually move; instead, it provides the energy that allows things to move. It's like the axle of an old-fashioned cart: it remains very stable, and so makes it possible for the wheel to move. Like this, our foundation always remains very calm and quiet, yet it sends forth

---

7. Three Treasures (三寶): In their outer aspect, the Three Treasures are the Buddha, the Dharma, and the Sangha. Buddha means both the historical Buddha, as well as this fundamental enlightened essence. Dharma means both ultimate truth, and the truth taught by the Buddha. Sangha in its broadest sense means the community of great practitioners, both lay and monastic. These are also considered to have an inner aspect as well.

이 말을 왜 되풀이 하느냐고 여러분이 그러시겠지만 이렇게 되풀이를 해도 여러분은 이론으로만 알고 머리로만 알아서 깊은 데로(가슴을 짚어 보이시며) 바로 통신이 되질 않고 있습니다. 깊이 통신이 돼서 사대(四大)[2]가 움죽거리질 않고, 항상 머리로 굴려서 몸을 움죽거리게 되니 그것이 아쉬운 것입니다. 그래서 항상 말을 되풀이하게 됩니다. 여러분이 요만큼 알면 나도 요만큼밖에 모릅니다. 여러분이(양 팔을 벌려 보이시고) 이만큼 알면 나도 이만큼 알게 되구요. 여러분이 바다와 같다면, 나도 바다와 같은 것입니다.

그래서 움죽거리지 않으면서도 힘을 배출해 줄 수 있는 자(自)의 근본, 그 자의 근본에서 마음을 내는 것, 그 마음 내는 것에 따라 움죽거리는 것, 이것이 자성삼보이고 이것이 불법승입니다. 따라서 자성삼보에 귀의한다는 건 자기한테 자기가 귀의하는 거예요. 각자 자기 자성한테 삼보가 있는 것이니까요.

---

2. **사대(四大)**: 불교에서는 사람의 몸이 지,수,화,풍이라는 네 가지 물질적 요소로 성립되었다 보고 있으므로, 사대란 곧, 인간의 신체를 일컬음.

great energy. Through this energy, everything in the universe is ceaselessly working and changing, beyond time and space, without stopping for even a millisecond.

You may wonder why I repeat this point so often. I keep bringing it up because many of you have only an intellectual understanding of it. You've mistaken theoretical knowledge for actually connecting with this deep essence that's within you [pointing to her heart.] You're trying to make things happen by using your head and moving your body, instead of communicating the situation to this place deep inside and then acting from there. This is such a shame, and it's why I keep repeating myself — if you understand only a little bit, then I also only understand a little bit. If you know this much [holding her arms wide], then I also know that much! If you are a great ocean, then I also am a great ocean.

So, the Three Treasures of inherent nature are these: this unmoving source of infinite energy, the foundation of our present consciousness; the raising of thoughts from this foundation; and the movement and functioning that result from these thoughts. These are also Buddha, Dharma, and

그러면 **계정혜**(戒定慧)[3]는 어디에 붙어 돌아가는가? 자성삼보에 귀의했으면 바로 자기가 들이고 내는 행(行)을 어떻게 해야만이 계라고 할 수 있을까? 항상 제가 이런 말을 하죠? 들이고 내는 것도 네놈이고, 움죽거리는 것도 네놈이요, 보는 것도 네놈이요, 듣는 것도 네놈이요, 가고 오는 것도 네놈이요, 똥싸고 밥 먹는 것도 네놈이요, 자는 것도 네놈이요, 모든 게, 일거수일투족이 다 네놈이 하는 거다 라구요. 나무는 제 뿌리가 있기 때문에 살아가는 거예요. 움죽거리는 전체가 다 그러하니 모든 거를, 즉, 정(定)에다가 모아야 진짜 정이 되죠. 그러기 때문에 **계향**(戒香)[4] 할 때에도 그렇고 계정혜 할 때도 그렇고 똑같은 이치입니다.

---

3. 계정혜(戒定慧): 불도(佛道)에 들어가는 세가지 요체인 계율, 선정, 지혜를 줄여서 이르는 말. 계(戒)는 몸과 입과 뜻으로 나쁜 짓을 하지 않고 선을 행하는 것, 정(定)은 어지럽게 흩어진 마음을 한곳에 모아 안정되게 머무는 것, 혜(慧)는 미혹을 깨뜨리고 진리를 깨닫기 위하여 사제(四諦), 십이연기(十二緣起), 진여(眞如)의 실상 등을 진중히 관하여 불법의 이치를 확실하게 체득하는 일.

4. 계향(戒香): 안과 밖에서 일어나는 모든 부딪힘을 자신의 탓으로 돌리면서, 부드러운 말과 행을 함으로써 화목을 도모할 줄 아는 것을 말함.

the *Sangha*.[8] Thus, taking refuge in the Three Treasures also means taking refuge in yourself. This is because the Three Treasures all exist within our inherent nature.

Then, what about keeping the *precepts,* practicing *samadhi,* and gaining *wisdom*?[9] How are these attained and practiced in the context of relying upon the Three Treasures of inherent nature? As I'm always saying, everything is coming directly from your inherent nature: it's you, true self, that's receiving and producing everything; it's you that's moving this body; it's you that's seeing; it's you that's hearing; it's you that's going and coming, that's eating and excreting, sleeping and waking up. It's you that's doing every single thing. A tree has its root, and is alive because of that root. Our every movement happens because of our root. So, no matter what

---

8. Sangha: Traditionally this refers to ordained monks and nuns, but it can also mean the entire community of Buddhist believers.

9. Precepts, Samadhi, and Wisdom(戒定慧)**:** Traditionally described as the Threefold Training, these are aimed at putting an end to desire, hatred, and delusion. Precepts represent virtue and morality, samadhi represents transcendental awareness, and wisdom is this awareness in action.

그래서 이 모든 것을 이렇게 해야만 우선은 자신에게 누(累)가 되지 않게 되는 것이고, 또 부처님 도량에 누가 되지 않게 하는 것이고, 은사나 사제, 사형한테 또 누가 되지 않는 겁니다. 스님네들은 물론이요, 여러분도 역시 마찬가지입니다. 여러분 각자 스스로에게 누가 되게 한다면 가정이 다 누가 되게 되는 거죠. 안 그렇습니까? 한 가정에 한 사람이 누가 되게 한다면 가정 전체에 누가 되는 것입니다. 부모까지도 자식까지도 말입니다.

그러하니까 모든 것을 내 탓으로 돌리세요. 바깥에서 들어오는 것도, 그것이 좋은 것이든 나쁜 것이든 분별하지 말고 모두 내 탓으로 돌리세요. 안에서 일어나는 것도, 적절한 이유가 있어 일어난다 하더라도 내 탓으로 돌리세요. 남편을 원망하지 말고 아내를 원망하지 말고, 자식을 원망하지 말고, 부모를 원망하지 말고 모든 거를 내 탓으로 돌리십시오.

you confront, if you focus everything on one place — your fundamental mind — this becomes true samadhi, precepts, and wisdom. This is what's called the "fragrance of precepts, samadhi, and wisdom."

Approach everything by entrusting it to your fundamental mind; then, you won't end up causing problems for yourself, your teacher, the temple, or your fellow practitioners. This is how sunims practice as well. If you do something that causes problems for yourself, that action also ends up causing hardships for your entire family, doesn't it? If one person in a family gets involved in something negative, the entire family feels it, including their parents and children.

So, view everything that confronts you as something that you helped create. No matter whether it comes from outside or arises from inside, whether it's good or bad, unconditionally accept it as something you have made. Even when you clearly know who or what caused those troubles, view them as something you've made, and entrust the whole situation to your foundation. Don't blame your husband, don't blame your wife, don't blame your children, and don't blame your

그건 왜냐하면, 못났든지 잘났든지 내가 이 세상에 났기 때문입니다. 바로 내가 이 자리에 있기 때문입니다. 내 탓으로 돌리라고 하면 '내가 뭐 잘못한 게 있어야 내 탓으로 돌리지,' 이렇게 말씀들 하시겠지만 내가 있기 때문에 상대가 있는 것이지, 내가 없다면 무슨 상대가 있겠습니까? 그러기 때문에 내 탓이라는 겁니다.

모든 걸 나에게 돌려놓고, 근본에 다 놔서 그게 입력이 되어, 그 입력된 게 다시 바깥으로 나오게 되면 법이 됩니다. 그냥 머리로 생각해서 나오는 대로 지껄이는 것은 법이 아닙니다.

그래서 이 마음도리를 공부하는 사람들은 아주 입이 무거워지고, 말이 적어지는 것입니다. 그러면서도 안으로 매사를 굴려서 근본에 맡기기 때문에 입력이 돼가지고 다시 현실로 나오는 거지요. 이렇게 그대로 법이 되니 그대로 걸림이 없다 이런 뜻입니다.

parents. Entrust it all as something that you've caused. Whether things are going well or badly, you experience everything that's happening in your life because you are here. Now, some of you are saying, "Why should I blame myself when I didn't do anything wrong?!" However, think about this: Because you exist, others exist. If you weren't here, how could other's actions affect you? This is why I say to take everything as something that you have made.

If you take everything as something that you've created, and then let it go deep within you, such that it connects with your foundation, later it will come back out as something new. When you connect with your foundation like this, what you input comes back out according to the intention you input it with and has the power to move the material world in that direction. But when your thoughts just spill out of your mouth, this connection isn't made.

For this reason, people who are determined to realize their foundation hold their tongues and become quiet. They return every single thing inwardly and entrust it all to their foundation. Having been deeply input in this way, those

정신계를 거쳐서 물질계로 나오니까 그것은 걸림이 없지만, 물질계에서 물질계로 그냥 나가게 되면 그건 항상 걸리고 사고가 생기고 이탈을 하게 되고 망종이 생기고 불화가 생기곤 합니다. 그럴 때마다 온통 이런 문제들을 어떻게 다 대치를 하시렵니까?

여러분이 이 마음 하나를 잘 해서 안으로 굴려 바깥으로 나오게 할 수 있는 그런 법신(法身)이 되신다면, 일상생활은 물론이거니와 여러 가지로 편리한 점이 한두 건이 아닙니다.

situations are communicated into their foundation, and through this they manifest back into the world in a changed form. When people input the things they encounter like this, those things all change for the better; thus, nothing they encounter can hinder or derail them. What could oppress you when everything you entrust to this spiritual dimension is sent back into the material realm in a more harmonious form?

However, when problems occur, many people just react directly to those, and run around looking for solutions in the material realm. Unless you first entrust things to your foundation, nothing will go right. You'll lose your direction, accidents will happen, and you'll get caught up in hatreds and feuds. The minds of some of those around you will become darker and darker, and leading a normal life will become impossible. Do you think you can solve all of these things through your intellect and sweat? When you're able to truly return and entrust everything you encounter to your foundation, such that what you input changes and manifests back into the world, then your life will become very relaxed and many problems will cease to be.

이 세상 일체 만물만생이 이심전심으로써 다 연결이 돼 있습니다. 왠 줄 아십니까? 여러분 몸 속에 천차만별의 모습, 여러분이 수억 겁을 거치면서 진화해서 창조되어온 그 지나간 세월의 모습들이 여러분 몸 속에 다 있기 때문입니다. 그래서 이 모습이 바로 '나'이니만큼 모든 만물만생이 '나' 아님이 없는 것이죠.

여러분이 각자 자기만 아는 비밀이 있다고 하지만, 보이지 않는 공법(空法)에서는 사실 비밀이 없습니다. 내가 '보이지 않는 공법'이라고 하는 이유는 육안으론 볼 수 없는 세계에서 항상 모든 게 통신이 되고 있기 때문입니다. 그래서 물질세계에서는 비밀이 있다고 하지만 무(無)의 세계에서는 비밀이 없다고 하는 것입니다.

All lives and things in the universe are connected with each other, communicating heart to heart. Do you know why this is? Within your body right now is every level of existence that you have ever experienced, as you've evolved over billions of eons. There's nothing in the universe that you haven't been, and all of those same forms exist within you right now: every single one of those is "me."

You might think that you have secrets unknown to anyone else, yet in the unseen realm of the Dharma, there are no secrets. I use the expression "unseen realm of the Dharma," because we can't see it with our physical eyes, and yet through it, every single thing is always freely communicating with everything else. Secrets may exist in the material realm, but in this nonmaterial realm, everything is known. Because nothing is secret, because nothing is withheld, every single thing you do is automatically recorded within your foundation. Everyone desperately needs to know this.

"The fragrance of the precepts" means taking everything that arises — from within you or outside of you, whether it's something about your

이렇듯 비밀이 없기 때문에, 그러한 내가 해 나가는 하나하나 그 자체가 근본자리에 다시 자동적으로 입력이 된다는 사실을 여러분은 아셔야 됩니다.

계향(戒香)이란 안에서 일어나는 거나 바깥에서 들어오는 거나, 가정에서 일어나는 거나, 직장에서 일어나는 거나 모든 걸 내 근본자리에다 입력을 해서 스스로 나오게 만들어야 이루어집니다. 그래야 내 자신은 물론 모두가 화목해지고 한마음[5]으로 돌아가게 되니까요. 그러질 않고 그냥 입에서 나오는 대로 "차라리 얼른 돌아가셨으면 좋겠어." "어휴! 저놈의 자식, 저거 차라리 눈에 안 띄었으면 좋겠어."라는 말을 아무 거리낌 없이 하게 된다면, 서로 화목하게 해결이 되기는커녕 해만 더 끼치게 되는 거죠. 과거로부터 쭉 인연을 맺어서 여기까지 온 우리는 모두 한 가족인데 그렇게 해서야 되겠습니까? 그런 식으로 한다면, 그렇게 될 수밖에는 없습니다.

---

5. 한마음: '한'이란 광대무변함, 일체가 하나로 합쳐진 것을 뜻하며, 한마음이란 만질 수도 없고 보이지도 않으며, 시공간을 초월하여, 시작도 끝도 없는 근본마음을 말함. 또한, 만물만생의 마음이 삼천대천세계와 서로 연결되어 하나로 돌아가는 것을 의미하기도 함. 다시 말해서, 한마음은 우주 전체와 그 속에서 살고 있는 일체 생명들의 근본마음과 그 마음들이 하나로 돌아가는 작용을 다 포함하고 있음.

family or your job or whatever — and returning it all to your foundation. In this way, the situation will manifest in a more harmonious, healthy form. When you can do this, you'll feel at peace with yourself and all other people as well.

However, if you speak without restraint about every little irritation, "She is so difficult!" or "That son of a ....!," this will actually make things worse for you than if you had made the effort to work things out harmoniously. Through the karmic connections created over innumerable lives, you and everyone else are all one family, so should you really be behaving like this? If you continue to think and act harshly towards each other, when will this cycle ever end? So take everything and input it harmoniously into this inner foundation; handled in this way, it will manifest harmoniously back into the material world. That which comes back out will have the power to move the world. It will protect you, it will smooth out the rough spots in your path, and it will give you opportunities to solve whatever difficulties you encounter, allowing you to move forward freely.

When you can thoroughly entrust everything to your foundation, and can remain focused on

그러니 모든 걸 안에다가 입력을 해서 바깥으로 물질세계로 나오게끔 둥글게 응용하도록 하세요. 그러면 모두 그게 법이 돼서 여러분을 지켜줄 거고, 여러분 길이 험악하더라도 험악치 않게 되고, 어떤 걸림이 오더라도 걸리지 않고 나갈 수 있는 계기가 될 것입니다.

그리고 모든 것을 내 근본자리에 일임하여 들이고 낼 때 마음을 한데 모아 정(定)으로써 하신다면 정향(定香)이 됩니다. 그러면 심봉을 완전히 뿌리 박았기 때문에 어디 내세워도 흔들리지 않게끔 됩니다. 따라서 정향이 되면 계향도 잘 되는 것이죠. 계(戒)는 안으로 모든 걸 굴려놓아야 잘 지켜지는 것이지, 그렇지 않으면 아무리 해도 오계(五戒)도 못 지켜요. 여러분 생각해보세요, 오계나 지킬 수 있는지. 오계에도 술 먹지 말라, 살생하지 말라, 거짓말하지 말라, 도둑질하지 말라, 이성 간에 도둑질 하지 말라, 뭐 이런 걸로 모두 되어 있는데 쉬운 거 같아 보여도 정(定)으로써 안으로 들이고 내지 않는다면 전혀 지킬 수 없습니다. 하지만 모든 것을 내 안으로 넣게 되면, 남의 생명도 내 생명과 다르지 않으니 일부러 해코지 하는 일이 없게 되며, 당연히 내 몸 상하게 하는 일도 하지 않게 되는 겁니다.

this foundation in all the things you do, this is called "the fragrance of Samadhi." At this point, what I call the "pillar of mind" has firmly taken root within you, so you remain unshaken in any circumstances. Thus, if you are able to realize the "fragrance of samadhi," the "fragrance of precepts" isn't difficult. When you return everything inwardly like this, keeping the precepts isn't a problem.

However, without doing this, it's impossible to uphold even the five basic precepts. Please think carefully about this. Do you think you can keep the five precepts without entrusting everything inwardly? These are the precepts of not drinking alcohol, lying, stealing, engaging in improper sexual behavior, or killing. If you're not trying to do things through your fundamental mind, if you're not acting from that place and inputting into that whatever arises, then you won't be able to keep even these precepts. When you return everything inwardly, to your foundation, you'll realize that others' lives are also your life, so you won't intentionally do anything that harms others. Returning things like this also ends up saving you from harm as well.

그런데 마음이 바깥으로 떠돌게 된다면, 정(定)에 들지를 않아요. 따라서 이 중심이, 심봉이 완벽하게 자리를 잡지 못했기 때문에 일체를 들이고 내는 데에 손상이 오죠. 뿌리가 완전히 자리를 잡지 못했기 때문에 여러분이 살아나가시면서 어떤 어려운 일이 닥치게 되면, '아이고!' 하고 겁이 턱턱 나고 그냥 안절부절 못하게 되는 겁니다. 안에서 일어나는 것도 그렇고, 바깥에서 들어오는 것도 그렇고, 자식들의 일도 그렇고, 부모의 일도 그렇습니다. 그냥 갈팡질팡 하게 되는 거죠. 그러면 이 주인공[6] 찾는 것도 말입니다, 그냥 아리송하게 됩니다. "그거, 주인공 불러봤던들 그냥 그렇더라." 이렇게 되는 거죠. 하하하. 그러니 말입니다. 이게 (가슴을 짚어 보이시며) 완벽하게 서서 자리를 완벽하게 잡아야, 들이고 내는 대로 입력이 되고, 입력이 돼야 현실로 되 나오게 되는 겁니다. 이게 돌아서 말입니다.

---

6. 주인공(主人空): 우리 모두 스스로 갖추어 가지고 있는 근본마음으로 일체 만물만생의 근본과 직결된 자리. 나를 존재하게 하고, 나를 움직이게 하며, 내 모든 것을 관장하는 참 주인이므로 주인(主人)이며, 매 순간 쉴 사이 없이 변하고 돌아가 고정된 실체가 없으므로 비어 있다고 할 수 있기 때문에 빌 공(空)자를 써서, 주인공(主人空)이라 함.

Nevertheless, if your mind wanders around after external things, you can't deeply enter into this meditative awareness, and so the pillar of mind isn't able to become completely grounded. This lack of a secure footing damages your ability to receive and send out everything through your fundamental mind.

When this pillar of mind is unsettled, you become scared and nervous when you encounter difficulties. There's an underlying nuance of fear and confusion that pervades your experiences, whether it's something arising from the inside or the outside, or whether it's a problem with your children or your parents. Everything about your fundamental mind, *Juingong*,[10] will seem more vague and confusing. "I called out to Juingong, but nothing happened." Should I laugh or cry when

---

10. Juingong (主人空): Pronounced "ju-in-gong." Juin (主人) means the true doer or the master, and gong (空) means "empty." Thus Juingong is our true nature, our true essence, the master within that is always changing and manifesting, without a fixed form or shape.

Daehaeng Sunim has compared Juingong to the root of the tree. Our bodies and consciousness are like the branches and leaves, but it is the root that is the source of the tree, and it is the root that sustains the visible tree.

그런데 사람들은 "나는 선원에 다닌 지 몇 해가 됐네, 이 공부한 지 몇 해가 됐네." 이럽니다. 단 석 달 한 것만도 못한 사람이 많은데 말입니다. 이건 심봉이 완전히 자리를 잡지 못했기 때문에 그런 겁니다. 이 문제들을 어떻게 해결해야만 되겠습니까? 머리로만 굴려서 하는 거라면 얼마나 좋겠습니까마는 이건 그런 게 아닙니다. 그런데도 머리로다 굴려서 이거를 다 알았다고 하면서, "나는 스님이 말씀하시는 것 다 이해하고 있고, 어떤 거 하나 빼놓지 않고 다 내 머리에 들어 있어."라며 자부합니다. 그러고는 이제 여기도 뜸하게 나오시는 분들도 계실 겁니다. 그런데 머리로다 굴려서 아는 건 진짜 아는 게 아닙니다. 실천을 한 발짝도 떼어 놓지 못하거든요. 그러니까 발버둥치죠.

people say things like this? You have to firmly raise this pillar of mind, and completely grab hold of it. If you can do this, then the thoughts you give rise to will naturally be input, and will manifest into the world.[11] Even though you may have been coming here for years, if your pillar of mind isn't deeply settled, your practice may be no more developed than that of someone who has been coming here for a few months. If this applies to you, what should you do about it? What should you do to grow and deepen your practice? Wouldn't it be nice if you could solve this with your intellect? But this isn't something that belongs to the realm of thoughts. Nonetheless, some of you are doing exactly this, and think you know everything about our fundamental mind. Just because you have some ideas about it doesn't mean that you truly know the real thing.

You all probably know someone like this: they feel confident in their thoughts and opinions

---

11. You have to input unconditionally and harmoniously, with the well-being of all in mind. If you're trying to input while still clinging to some desire or fear, or with greed or hatred, things won't go well for you, nor will your pillar of mind become grounded.

인생이 어디에서 와서 어디로 가는 지도 모르고, 지금 내가 무엇을 어떻게 중심을 잡아서 해야 하는지도 모르는 거예요. 모든 거를 어떻게 대처할 수 있는지 그것조차도 아리송한 거죠. 그래 가지고야 어떻게 이 우주를 삼킬 수 있는, 과거 현재 미래, 삼천대천세계를 다 삼킬 수 있는 공부를 할 수 있겠습니까? 초발심이 났을 때 내가 자리라도 완벽하게 잡아야죠.

사람들 사는 것도 그래요. 가정을 이룰 때 내가 그 안에서 완전히 자리를 잡아야 가정이 화목하고 식구들도 다 편안해지지 내가 자리를 잡지 못하면 어떻게 모두가 화목할 수 있겠습니까? 어떻게 걱정 없이 살 수 있겠습니까?

이렇듯 내 몸 속의 생명들도, 중생들도 다 한마음으로 자리가 잡혀야 이게 뿌리가 내리고, 뿌리가 내려야 바로 여유 있고 유유하게 열매를 맺을 수 있는 겁니다. 바로 거기에서 무르익어 그것을 남들에게 줄 수도 있고, 또, 주면서도 항상 중심은 거기에 그대로 있기 때문에, 그 불종자(佛種子)가 남아 있기 때문에, 근기로써, 모든 지혜로써 들이고 내는 데에 손색이 없게 됩니다. 그렇게 돼야만이 이제 정(定)에 들었다고 하는 겁니다.

about what I'm teaching, and so think that they've truly reached that level. They mistake thoughts for experience and the ability to apply that experience. As time goes by, they gradually stop coming to the temple. However, when problems arise, they struggle and squirm, because they haven't made any effort at putting their understanding into practice. They don't know where they've come from or where they're going. They lose their direction, and don't know how to handle the things in their life. How could such a person engage in the spiritual practice that can swallow the entire universe, as well as the Dharma-realm, and the past, present, and the future?

If you're aspiring to practice, you have to first thoroughly ground yourself in relying upon and entrusting everything to your foundation. Living with a family is the same way: only when you are deeply settled in your role and responsibilities will your family be harmonious and peaceful. If your attention is always somewhere else, how can your family thrive?

Like this, the lives within your body also need to be firmly settled and working as one. They need to be rooted in this. Then there will

이와 같이 정(定)에 들었다 하면 이 뿌리가 완벽하게 내렸기 때문에 바로 어딜 가도 내 자리요, 누구를 봐도 나 아님이 없음이요, 어떤 아픔을 봐도 내 아픔 아님이 없음이요, 어떠한 벌레를 봐도 내 생명 아님이 없음이요, 모든 것이 나 아님이 없으니 어찌 자비가 그 속에서 저절로 우러나오지 않겠습니까? 가짜 사랑이 아니라, 껍데기 사랑이 아니라 아주 진실한 자비 말입니다.

여러분도 항상 그렇게 생활하시고 계시죠? 보면 생각나고 생각나면 움죽거리고 이게 들이고 내는 겁니다. 그런데 이 들이고 낼 때에 지혜로운 마음으로 들이고 내느냐, 아니면 아까 말 한대로 지혜롭지 못하게 머리로 그냥 굴려서 들이고 내느냐, 어떻게 하느냐에 따라 그 결과는 천지차이입니다.

be a deep quiet and peace that will naturally bear fruit. When this fruit ripens, you will be able to give it to others as well. Even though you give it to others, your center remains just as it is.

To put it another way, the seed of Buddha remains just as it is, so you'll be able to completely send out and receive everything through your foundation, using every kind of wisdom and profound ability. Only when you can do this, can it be said that you are in the state of samadhi.

Samadhi means that you are completely rooted in this foundation. So, everywhere you go, that is your place, every person you see is also yourself, the pain you witness is your own pain, and even insects are your own body. Every single thing is yourself, so compassion naturally arises for them all. This isn't forced or artificial, it is utterly genuine compassion.

When we see something, thoughts arise, and according to those thoughts, we move and act. This is "receiving and sending forth." Now, the question is this: are we doing this from our foundation, with wisdom, or are we doing it from our head and our intellect? The corresponding results will be as different as heaven and earth.

여러분이 그렇게 마음공부[7]를 못 한다면, 그래서 머리로만 굴려 내놓는다면 우리나라뿐만 아니라 지구, 세계 전체, 다른 행성들에게도 폐해가 말이 아닙니다.

우주는 우주대로, 은하계의 모든 별성들은 때가 다 지나면은 껍데기가 저절로 떨어지고 알맹이만 추려져서 바로 블랙홀이 재생산을 하게 되죠. 이 모두가 사람이 살고 있는 섭리와 똑같습니다. 그런데 어떤 게 문제냐? 보세요. 여러분이 이렇게 마음 도리를 공부하시게 된 것은 우리가 하고 싶다고 해서 되는 것도 아니요, 하기 싫다고 해서 그만둬서도 안 되는 도리입니다. 벌써 이 천지간의 이치가 있어서 이렇게 하는 겁니다. '이 어려운 시기에 너, 이 공부를 해서 모든 걸 대처하라.' 이런 소임을 여러분한테다 준 것입니다. 이게 그냥 의도적으로 아니면 그냥 우연히 이렇게 하게 된 것이 아니라, 이건 수억 겁 년 전부터 지금까지 진화해 오면서 이렇게 된 인연들이기 때문입니다. 따라서 이런 저런 이유로 마음공부를 그만둬서는 안됩니다.

---

7. 마음공부: 자유인이 되기 위해 마음이 어떻게 작용하는지를 배우고, 배운 것을 실제로 생활 속에서 활용하고 실험해 보면서 경험하고 체험해 가며 알아가는 모든 과정을 말함.

If you're unable to rely upon your fundamental mind, and instead try to use your intellect to handle everything, the harm to we humans, to the planet, and even to other planets will be incredibly serious. What is true on the human scale is also true on the universal scale. Even the stars in the sky shed their shells when the time comes, and only their essence remains. After this essence is sifted out, it's born anew through a black hole. This process is exactly the same as what we experience at the human level.

By the way, do you know that there are definite reasons why you've encountered this practice of learning to rely upon your fundamental mind? This spiritual practice isn't something that you can do just because you want to, nor is it something that you can quit just because you want to. There is a very deep principle that has led you to this practice. In this difficult era, all of you were given the assignment of taking care of everything through your fundamental mind. This is neither planned nor accidental. It has arisen from the karma and affinities that you have created as you've evolved over billions of years. So you

그러면 어떠한 거를 어떻게 대처를 하느냐? 예를 들어, 내 가정에서 어떤 일이 생기게 되면 나와 내 자녀들과 부모, 모두의 마음과 더불어 내 몸뚱이 속에 있는 이 생명들도 다 한마음이 되어야 합니다. 이렇게 모두 한마음이 됐다가 벌어지면은, 다시 말해, 무의 세계에서 근본자리를 통해 하나로 응축되었던 에너지가, 그 진수가 분출되어 나오게 되면, 물질로 되어 있는 유의 세계에서 실제로 물리적인 작용을 하게 되는 것입니다. 그런데 그 힘이 대단하여 한두 사람 마음으로는 풀 수 없는 어떠한 큰 문제가 생겼을 때, 많은 사람들의 마음을 하나로 모을 수 있으며, 그 문제에 대처할 수 있게 해주는 겁니다.

must not avoid practicing, giving one excuse after another.

Then, how should you handle things? When something happens in your family, for example, you, your children, your parents, and even the lives inside your body should all become one through your foundation. If all become one mind, energy radiates outward and helps take care of people's minds. To explain it one way, once all those minds become one through the foundation, it's as if they all become condensed into an extract. When this condensed essence bursts forth from the nonmaterial realm into the physical realm, it takes the form of material energy that can function in and affect this realm. Sometimes, there are problems so severe that even working through our foundation, one or two people alone can't take care of them. At those times, many people all together have to entrust the situation to their foundation; then those problems can be solved.

관세음이 될 때는 관세음이 되고, 지장이 되어야 할 때는 지장이 되고, 칠성이 되어야 할 때는 칠성이 되고, 용신(龍神)이 되어야 할 때는 용신이 되고, 지신(地神)이 되어야 할 때는 지신이 되면서, 자유자재로 작용을 하게 되는 거죠. 고정되어 있는 에너지가 아니기 때문에 필요에 따라 원하는 대로 그냥 모두가 천차만별로 갈라져서 활용을 하게 돼 있습니다.

이와 같이 완벽하게 활용을 하기 위해서는 계정혜(戒定慧)가 당연히 완벽하게 돼야겠죠. 그래야 **해탈향**(解脫香)[8], **해탈지견향**(解脫知見香)[9]까지 이르게 되니까요.

---

8. 해탈향(解脫香): 안으로는 다가오는 모든 것을 주인공에 일임하고 믿고 맡겨 놓음으로써, 억겁에 걸쳐 자신이 지어놓은 업의 과보라든가 죄업에 묶인 것이 풀어지는 것을 말하며, 밖으로는 인연되어 다가오는 모든 생명들을 보는 대로 무명의 굴레에서 전부 벗어나게 해주는 것을 말함. 즉 무명에 얽매여서 헤어나지 못하는 중생들의 묶여있는 마음을 다 풀어주어, 그들이 살아가면서 지혜로워지고 진화를 함으로써 지금의 모습에서 벗어나 차제(次第)에 보다 높은 차원의 모습으로 형성될 수 있도록 이끌어 주는 것을 일컬음.

9. 해탈지견향(解脫智見香): 만물만생의 생명과 몸과 아픔을 모두 자신의 생명과 몸과 아픔으로 여길 수 있고, 도처가 자신의 도량이며, 일체 제불 보살들과 둘이 아니게 돌아가고, 일체 삼라만상 대천세계와도 전부 하나가 되기도 하고, 수만으로 펼쳐지기도 하면서 작용을 할 수 있는 것을 말함. 가장 지극한 깨달음인 구경(究竟)경지에 이르러서 자유스럽게 과거, 현재, 미래는 물론이거니와 우주 삼천대천세계를 한번에, 한생각에, 찰나에 돌아볼 수 있고, 들을 수 있고, 같이 응할 수 있고, 통할 수 있는 경지를 일컬음.

If the situation calls for the *Bodhisattva*[12] of Compassion, this energy becomes *Avalokitesvara*.[13] If the Bodhisattva of Manifestation is needed, it becomes *Ksitigarbha*.[14] When people need the Seven Star Spirit, the Dragon Spirit, or the Earth Spirit, our foundation manifests as such. Your foundation freely manifests in whatever form or manner is necessary. That energy doesn't all have the same form or "wavelength." According to the need, it changes and splits in an infinite variety of ways, and functions in harmony with the circumstances.

In order to fully use your fundamental mind like this, you must have realized the "fragrance" of the precepts, samadhi, and wisdom. You must further realize the spiritual state that we call the

---

12. Bodhisattva: In the most basic sense a Bodhisattva is a manifestation of Buddha, which helps save beings and also uses the non-dual wisdom of enlightenment to help them awaken for themselves.

13. Avalokitesvara Bodhisattva (觀世音菩薩): The Bodhisattva of compassion, who hears and responds to the cries of the world, and delivers unenlightened beings from suffering.

14. Ksitigarbha Bodhisattva (地藏菩薩): The guardian of the earth who is devoted to saving all beings from suffering, and especially those beings lost in the hell realms.

우리가 과거, 현재, 미래, 이 삼세를 뒤로 돌아가려면 돌아갈 수 있고, 앞으로 갈려면 갈 수 있고, 현재도 공(空)해서 어떤 걸로라도 내가 될 수 있는 그런 경지에 이르러야, 즉 여래가 되어야 이 우주의 태양력뿐만 아니라, 블랙홀이나 우주 전체의 다른 별성들의 문제들도 대처할 수 있는 겁니다.

그런데 옛날부터, 내가 스무 살이 되기 전부터 어느 나라가, 세계가 멸망하느니 마느니 하는 이런 말이 있었습니다. 그런데 부처님께서 이런 말씀을 하셨습니다.

> "보는 것도 도가 아니다. 보기만 하고 해결할 줄 모르면서 예언을 하는 것은 소인이 하는 일이다. 듣기만 하고 해결 못 한다면 그건 도(道)가 아니다. 천이통(天耳通)[10]도 도가 아니요, 천안통(天眼通)도 도가 아니요, 타심통(他心通)도 도가 아니요, 신족통(神足通)도 도가 아니요, 숙명통(宿命通)

---

10. 천이통(天耳通): 불가에서 말하는 **오신통**(五神通) 중의 하나로 듣는 사이 없이 들을 수 있는 능력을 말함. 그 밖에 오신통에는 천안통(天眼通), 타심통(他心通), 숙명통(宿命通), 신족통(神足通)이 포함됨. **천안통**(天眼通)은 보는 사이 없이 볼 수 있는 능력, **타심통**(他心通)은 다른 이의 마음을 아는 사이 없이 알 수 있는 능력, **신족통**(神足通)은 한 찰나에 가고 옴이 없이 가고 올 수 있는 능력, **숙명통**(宿命通)은 상대가 과거에 어떻게 살아 왔는지를 아는 사이 없이 알며, 미래에 어떻게 될 것인지 까지 아는 능력을 말함.

"fragrance" of being able to help free beings from attachments and ignorance. Beyond this is the level where you can manifest as needed, freely going back and forth among the past, present, and future as the occasion demands, manifesting as anything. Only when you have reached this state, that of the *Tathagata*,[15] can you handle the solar radiation of the sun, as well as the problems of other stars, black holes, and the universe.

When I was about eighteen or so, I first heard stories and predictions about the end of the world. However, as Shakyamuni Buddha said, "Just seeing isn't the Way. Focusing on seeing and making prophecies, while lacking the ability to change things, is the act of a small person." Being able to hear everything, yet remaining unable to resolve things, is not the Path. The power to hear everything is not the Path. The power to know the minds of others is not the Path. The power to go anywhere without moving your body is not the Path. And the power to know past and future

---

15. Tathagata: In one sense, Tathagata s just another name of the Buddha, meaning "Thus-come," but it also refers to the fully enlightened state that is able to both know and manifest with complete freedom.

도 도가 아니다. 단, 거기서 벗어나면 도이니라. 누진(漏盡)[11]이 되어야 모든 것을 다 살펴서 대처할 수 있고, 들일 수 있고 낼 수 있으며, 내도 줄지 않고 들여도 두드러지지 않느니라."

그 예언자들이 어떠한 사람들입니까? 한 분을 예를 들어 보면 여러분도 많이 들으셨으리라고 봅니다만, 노스트라다무스가 어떤 예언을 했다 이러죠. 그런데 말입니다, 그런 건 부처님이 가르치시는 것처럼 우리의 마음을 증득해서, 오신통(五神通)을 다 알아서 오신통에서도 벗어나 자유자재권을 얻은 사람의 말이 아닙니다. 그러니까 이런 예언은 마음 도리를 공부하는 사람한테 들켰다 하면은 그건 무효가 되는 거예요. 이 뜻을 잘 새겨야 됩니다.

---

11. 누진(漏盡): 일반적으로 마음이 어떤 대상이나 사물 및 상황에 끄달림으로 해서 일어나게 되는 모든 번뇌가 다 없어진 상태를 말함. 불가에서 말하는 오신통(五神通)에서 벗어나 그걸 자유스럽게 굴릴 수 있는 경지를 이름하여 누진이라 함.

lives is not the Path. Instead, the Path is found within the letting go of all attachments to those kinds of powers. You have to be completely free of all of these kinds of powers, then you'll be able to perceive everything and to take care of everything. At the stage where you are not caught by those, you can freely use them as needed. You can receive anything, and send forth anything. No matter how much you send forth, your foundation doesn't shrink, and no matter what or how much you receive, it doesn't increase.

So who are these people that are making prophecies? One person you've probably all heard of is Nostradamus. As you know, he predicted all kinds of different things. However, these sorts of prophecies aren't the words of a person who has realized the truth. They aren't the words of someone who has mastered and is unattached to the *five subtle powers*,[16] and who can use his or her fundamental mind to respond to any need. When someone who practices relying upon this

---

16. The five subtle powers(五神通)**:** These are the power to know past and future lives, the power to know other's thoughts and emotions, the power to see anything, the power to hear anything, and the power to go anywhere.

어떤 사람이 구름을 타고 다니면서 온갖 일을 다 했는데, 한 스님이 어느 날 가만히 보니까 그 사람이 또 구름을 타고 나가거든요. 그래, 그 놈을 쫓아가서 보니까 아, 그 놈이 못된 짓을 하는 거예요. 그래서 구름을 타고 가는 놈을 탁 막아서 못 가게 만들었죠. 내가 왜 이런 이야기를 하느냐? 세상의 멸망은 제가 알기로도 벌써 그 시기가 몇 번이나 왔다 지나갔습니다. 기는 놈 위에 나는 놈이 있기 때문이죠. 허허허. 이 도리를 체득한 사람이 '우리가 지금 멸망을 해서는 안되지 않겠느냐.'라는 마음을 낸 것입니다. 그러한 위기가 닥쳤더라도 우리가 순조롭게 살 수 있도록 전체가 마음을 모으면 되는데 왜 그렇게 하지 않습니까?

fundamental mind becomes aware of future events, they immediately start working on that situation, and so prophecies about those events become worthless. You really need to engrave what I'm saying in your heart.

There was a man who could ride clouds, and who was always traveling around here and there. One day a great practitioner perceived that the man was nearby, and decided to follow him and see what he was up to. The practitioner saw that the man was doing all kinds of bad things, and so he stopped him from being able to ride the clouds. Do you know why I'm telling you this? Because events that people like Nostradamus expected to be the apocalypse have already come and gone several times. People who make these kinds of predictions can't hold a candle to someone who has awakened to their fundamental mind and knows how to live from that place. When such people see a crisis approaching, they deeply input into their foundation the thought that we should not fall into chaos or go extinct. Even though such a disaster is facing us, if we all input the thought that we and the planet should live together in harmony, it will be so. Please give this a try.

지구의 지형이 벌여졌다가 오므라졌다가 다시 방향을 바꾸고, 이렇게 지형이 변경이 된다는 사실은 여러분도 잘 아시죠? 이 변경이 되는 것도 순조롭게 잘 리드해 가면서 변경이 된다면 이거는 걱정이 없습니다. 만물만생이 살아 있기에 움죽거리는 것이니까요. 흙도 살아 있고, 물도 살아 있고, 돌도 살아 있고, 다 살아 있기 때문입니다. 그래서 일본, 중국, 미국, 그 어디에서 이러한 움죽거림 때문에 어떠한 손색이 있다 하더라도 순조롭게 잘 리드해 간다면, 이건 결국 우리 전체가 숨을 쉬고 살 수 있게끔 해 주는 과정이기 때문에 큰 걱정은 없다는 거죠. 따라서 언제 어떻게 멸망한다는 식의 소리는 있을 수 없습니다. 아예 멸망이라는 말 자체가 변화무쌍하게 돌아가는 그 움직임 속에 붙지 않는다는 것입니다. 왜냐? 생명이란 애초에 지수화풍으로부터 나왔고, 그로부터 또 수많은 생명들이 생겨 진화하여 오늘날의 인간도 있게 됐습니다. 이 모든 것의 바탕이 되는 지수화풍이, 불종자가 없어지지 않기 때문입니다. 그러니 언제 멸망한다라는 소리에 개의치 마십시오. 이 멸망이라는 문제도 다 이렇게 넓고 지혜롭게 대처해 나갈 수 있는 마음들이 모이면 잘 해결해 나갈 수 있으니까요.

You already know that the surface of the Earth is always changing, don't you? It's always opening, crashing together, rising or falling, and changing direction. But if you could lead these changes so that they happen gently, then what would there be to worry about?

The land and all beings move because they are alive. Dirt is alive, water is alive, rocks are alive; everything is moving because it is alive. So even if someone predicts a cataclysmic disaster in China, Japan, or the U.S., if you can guide the ground so that those changes happen gradually, without large disruptions, what is there to worry about? In this way, human beings can find a way forward. This is why predictions about the end of the world have no meaning. The words, "the end of the human race," have no relevance in the varied and ever-changing panorama of life. Why? Because life arose from earth, water, fire, and air, and from those, countless beings evolved, including human beings. They live and evolve because the material basis of the four elements and the seed of Buddha-nature have always been present. These have never disappeared. So don't be bothered by talk that the world or civilization will

금성이나 화성이나 또는 목성이나 천왕성, 이런 데는 전부 생명체가 없다고들 하죠? 그러나 물이 있거나 흙이 있거나 하면은 바로 그것이 공기를 일으켜서 생명체가 생기게끔 돼 있습니다. 아주 펄펄 끓는 물이라고 해서 생명체가 없는 게 아닙니다. 펄펄 끓는 물이라도 완화되고, 종합이 되어 생명이 생기게끔 돼 있는 거죠. 이 심오하고 광대한 법을 불법이라고 합니다. 이 단어가 포함하고 있는 것이 얼마나 광대하고 미묘한지 모릅니다. 이걸 어느 특정 종교에 국한되어 있다고 생각한다든지, 머리 깎은 사람만이 불법을 공부하는 거라 생각해서는 안 됩니다. 지수화풍으로부터 일체 전부가 불(佛) 아닌 게 하나도 없어요. 풀 한 포기, 벌레 한 마리까지도 말입니다.

그런데 이러한 생명들이 시간이 지나면서 처해진 환경에 따라 '아휴! 참 이건 아쉽다. 요건 이렇게 됐으면 좋겠다!' 하는 생각이 들게 되거든요. 진화가 시작되는 겁니다. 그래서 여기까지도 올라 왔구요. '이렇게 네 다리로 엎드려 사는 게 참 힘들다. 난 서서 다녔으면 좋겠다.' 해서 여러분 모두 꼬리를 뗀 채 서서 다니지 않습니까? 그 꼬리가 붙어 있었던 자리는 아마 그대로 있을 겁니다.

be destroyed on such-and-such a day. If people work together through their inherent foundation to harmoniously and wisely take care of whatever arises, then even the destruction of the earth can be averted.

People usually say there's no life on planets like Mars, Venus, Jupiter, and Uranus, don't they? However, if there is water or soil, this will create air, and life will form. There are forms of life that live in even boiling water; even this can sustain and give rise to life. This profound and boundless truth is also called the Buddha-dharma. People can't imagine just how vast and how subtle this word is. The Buddha-dharma isn't limited to a particular religion or something that only Buddhist monks or nuns can study. From a bug to a blade of grass to the four elements, everything is Buddha.

According to their circumstances, those tiny living things began to change over time. They began to feel suffocated with the way they had been living and aspired to something better. In this way, they began to evolve and change. They got tired of walking around on four legs, and wanted to try walking on two legs, and so it happened. We even have the spot where the tail was attached.

이처럼 과거에 드러내고 살던 그 모습들이 여러분 육체 안에 고스란히 들어 있습니다. 생각하면 아주 심오하죠.

얼굴색도 아주 흰 사람이 있는가 하면, 붉은 사람이 있고, 또 검은 사람이 있는가 하면 누런 사람이 있습니다. 이런 것도 놓여진 환경에 따라 어떻게 살게 되는지가 다르다 보니, 자연히 지역별로 나뉘어져 살게 된 것입니다. 또한 개개인이 어떻게 반응하고 살았느냐에 따라 인연되어 모여지며 지망년(至亡年)[12]도 겪게 됩니다. 그래야 굵은 것은 추리고 나머지는 퇴비로 들어가 돌아 나올 테니까 말입니다. 다시 해서 다시 나오는 겁니다. 때때로 어느 지역이 전부 타 죽게 생겼다, 굶어 죽게 생겼다 하는 원인도 거기에 있다고 봅니다. 냉정하게 판단하면 말이지요. 불쌍하게 만드는 것도 자신들이요, 좋게 만드는 것도 자신들입니다. 다시 추려서 나올 때, 여기로 갈 거냐 저리로 갈 거냐 결정짓게 되는 것도 자신들입니다. 아주 죽는 게 아니에요.

---

12. 지망년(至亡年): 운수가 몹시 나쁜 해

Like this, all of the shapes of your past lives are within your body even now. This is so profound.

People have many different skin tones, don't they? There are people with very white complexions, there are people with reddish complexions, with black complexions, and with yellowish complexions. These are all the results of people living in different environments, which also led to natural differences between regions. On top of this, how people react to the things in their life causes them to gather together with people who have similar *karmic affinities*.[17] In the fullness of time, that karma manifests in the area where those people have gathered, and affects everyone there. Through this process, the "healthy" ones are selected, and the rotten ones are sent to the compost pile, so they can have a chance to start over. This is why, once in a while, you see such terrible catastrophes in certain areas, where it seems like nearly everyone starves to death, or is burned to death. This all happens as a result of the

---

17. Karmic Affinity(因緣): The connection or attraction between people or things, due to previous karmic relationships.

그런데요, 이것을 그냥 그대로 세상 변동이라 여기고, 그 일련의 과정 속에 고통 받는 사람들을 그저 닿는 대로 돕고 이렇게 살아야 되는데 그러질 않고, '네가 죄를 지었으니까 네가 그렇게 된 것은 당연해.'라고 생각하신다면 안 된다는 겁니다.

세상이 어떻게 돌고 도는지를 안다면 지금 그들이 나와 둘이 아님을 알아야 할 것입니다. 설사 상대가 단순히 불쌍한 처지에 있는 게 아니라, 강도라 할지라도 도둑놈이라 할지라도, 도둑질을, 강도질을 왜 하게 됐느냐부터 알아서 불쌍히 여겨서 선처를 베푸십시오. 그러한 마음을 자꾸 내야 여러분이 다시 추려져 나올 때 아주 과감하게 큰 인물로다가 태어날 수 있지 않겠습니까? 굶어 죽는 사람들에게 음식을 보낸다던가, 고통 받고 힘들어 하는 사람들을 위문 한다든가 하는 일들을 소홀히 해서는 안됩니다.

choices people have made and how they've reacted to things, to put it a bit bluntly. It's you that makes yourself pitiful, and it's you that can make yourself better. After this sorting, it's also you who decides where you'll be born again. Death is not the end.

Nonetheless, you should still help those people who are suffering and in pain as they are caught up in these changes. Do not dismiss their suffering, thinking "They deserve it; it's all the result of their own bad behavior." Understand how this world works, and realize that others are also a part of yourself.

Don't limit your compassion to just those who are suffering. Include even those who are behaving very badly; try to examine why they first did those things, and then direct your kindness there. If you keep raising such a kind and generous mind, when you come back into this world, it will be as a truly great person who is able to do much good for everyone. Don't neglect to give food to those who are hungry, nor comfort to those who are suffering.

By the way, if the Earth were to fall into disaster, not only would this cause serious trouble for human beings, it would also cause a lot of

그런데 지구가 망하면은 거기에 사는 사람뿐만 아니라 우주적으로 이게 다 지장이 초래됩니다. 다른 데도 다 한번 뒤집어져야 되는 문제가 생긴다고 봐야죠. 그런 일이 생기지 않도록 융통성 있게 대처를 해 나가야 합니다. 예를 들어, 한군데 인구가 너무 많으면 좀 넓은 데로 옮겨 살게 한다든가 말이죠. 세계인으로서 마음을 모아 연구를 하면, 어떠한 거든지 다 대처할 수 있다 이런 겁니다.

지구도 이제는 헐어져서 우리가 보수를 못 한다면은 속수무책으로 우리가 죽는다 이런 문제가 있습니다. 그런데 보수를 하게 되면 어떻게 보수를 해야 하느냐? 결과적으로 얘기 하자면 이 마음의 도리가 아니라면 보수를 할 수가 없습니다. 할래야 할 수도 없고 또 어찌저찌 보수를 했다고 치더라도 에너지가 없어서 유지 할 수가 없습니다. 살아갈 수가 없는 거죠. 우리 마음의 도리가 아니라면 허공에서 에너지를 흡수할 수가 없기 때문입니다. 그러면 과학자들이 어떻게 그 도리를 알아서 연구를 하느냐? 마음공부를 하는 사람들이 과학자들한테 내가 돼서 연구를 하게끔 마음이 하나가 되게 베풀어야 합니다.

problems for the universe as well. Disasters on the Earth will lead to great upheavals in other places. It's necessary to be flexible and respond with wisdom to ensure that these things don't happen. For example, if there are too many people in one place, then we can take measures to help them live in a more spacious area. If we, as citizens of the world, put our minds together to address the problems we face, we can take care of anything.

Things have now reached the stage where the Earth has become so worn out that if we can't repair it, we'll be watching helplessly as we die. So, what do we have to do? Ultimately, all the work we do has to be done through our fundamental mind. If we aren't doing it through our fundamental mind, no matter how hard we try, we won't be able to repair the Earth. And even if we somehow managed to make some repairs through ordinary means, there would be no energy to sustain those repairs. There would be no way to survive. Without being able to use our fundamental mind, we will not be able to absorb the energy that exists in the empty space all around us.

Without including this fundamental mind, scientists who study this kind of energy will be

마음은 고정됨이 없어서 백도 되고 천도 되고 만도 됩니다. 이렇게 정해진 바가 따로 없이 수없이 생겨나고 천차만별로 움직입니다. 이렇게 단 한 순간도 고정됨이 없으니 이름을 붙일 수도 없고 무엇을 했다라고 할 수도 없는 법이 마음법입니다. 그래서 다른 사람이 어떤 연구를 할 때, 연구하는 사람에게 마음을 모두 모아 내어주면 그 사람의 마음과 하나가 되어 돌아갈 수 있게 되는 겁니다. 이렇게 마음을 배출시키고 베풀어 준다면 앞을 못 보던 사람을 눈 뜨게 하고, 다리를 절며 걸었던 사람을 제대로 걷게 하는, 무한한 잠재력을 가지고 있는, 한계 없는 이 세상을 잘 이끌어 나갈 수 있는 그런 미묘한 법이 되지 않을까 생각합니다.

unable to truly make progress in their research. Thus, those people who practice relying upon their fundamental mind have to become one with scientists in order to help lead them to solutions that will benefit all of humanity.

Mind functions without limitation, so it can become a hundred, a thousand, or ten thousand It has no fixed essence, so it takes countless shapes and moves in an infinite number of different ways. Because it never remains the same for even an instant, names are meaningless, nor can we truly speak about anything we've done. So, when scientists are working on a particular area of research, if we raise the intention that their work should go well, then the energy of that combines with them and helps their research move forward. If we keep raising and sharing the energy of our foundation in this way, we'll achieve the infinite and incredibly powerful Dharma. It is utterly without limitation, and is subtle and profound beyond imagining. Through it the blind can see and the lame can walk. Truly, it can guide and sustain the entire world.

Yet, if we think, "There's nothing we can do about it," or "If that happens, human beings will

만약에 모두들 "우린 못해, 할 수 없어." "그렇게 되면 우린 멸망해서 죽을 거야!"라고 생각한다면 그렇게밖엔 될 수 없습니다. "지구가 멸망하면 죽을 테니깐 우리 굴이나 파고 들어가자!" 해서도 절대 안됩니다. 하하하! 그냥 몇 달, 몇 해 먹을 거 가지고 들어가서 우리나 살자 이러면은 나중에 벌레밖에는 못됩니다. 땅속에 사는 벌레밖에는 못돼요. 그리고 땅속도 어디 그게 땅속입니까? 지구가 어떻게 생긴 건데, 지금 공중에, 물 위에 떠 있는 거예요. 땅속으로 들어가 봤던 들, 위 아래도 없는 곳에 들어가봤던 들, 뭘 합니까? 거기 들어가면 얼마나 오래 살 것 같습니까? 지구가 망가졌는데 말입니다.

그러니까 그런 소소한, 죽기 싫어서 내는 소소한 생각은 마시고, '영원한 참다운 나'가 있다는 사실을 먼저 아십시오. '영원한 참다운 나'가 있기에, 그 종자 하나를 가지고도 세계를 다 먹일 수 있고, 또 그 종자가 되남아서 세계를 영원토록 먹일 수 있습니다. 우리는 이 광대한 법을 체득해야 됩니다.

be wiped out." then that's what will happen. Don't ever get caught up in the idea that some sort of apocalypse is coming and so you should hide deep underground in caves or bunkers. If you plan on trying to survive by storing up a few months or years of food and living underground, you'll end up being reborn as a burrowing insect or rodent.

Besides, does "under the ground" really have any meaning? Imagine the Earth as it floats in space. Even though you go into the ground, from this perspective, there's no difference between being on the surface or under it. There's no use in trying to live under the ground. If something is wrong with the planet, how much good is burrowing a few inches under the surface going to do you?

So don't let the fear of death cause you to waste your time with such trivial ideas. Instead, you need to come to know your eternal, true self. This true self exists. It is a single seed that can feed the entire world. It remains just as it is, without shrinking or decreasing, and can feed the whole world forever. We must each experience this incredible truth for ourselves, and make it our own.

하루는 어떤 분이 얘기 하길, 그 사람이 너무 아파 병원에 가니까 심장도 나쁘고 간도 나쁘고 황달도 심하고 당뇨도 심한데 연세가 있으시니까 어떻게 해볼 방도가 없다구요. 그러니까 그냥 입원해서 잘 자시고 그렇게 계시라고 하더랍니다. 통증이 심하다니깐 주사만 놓아 주고요. 그래서 그 사람이 어떤 생각이 들었냐 하면은 사람 사는 게 너무 허망하더랍니다. 허망해서 눈물이 한없이 흐르더랍니다. '야, 네가 이 몸뚱이를 형성시켰고, 또 이렇게 죽도록 아프게도 만들었으니 에라, 죽으려면 빨리 죽고 살려면 그냥 살아라. 너 알아서 해라.' 그러고는 그 길로 퇴원을 해서 집에 왔답니다. '에이그, 이 몸뚱이가 다 헐어져서 이젠 뭐 제대로 쓸 수도 없으니까 빨리 몸뚱이나 바꿔라. 네 마음대로 해라.' 이러고는 속 편히 며칠 지냈는데, 아, 통증이 없어지더랍니다. 하하하. 그 마음이 사대(四大)로 통신이 된 모양입니다. 그게 통신이 되니까 작용이 됐겠죠.

One day, an older man came and told me about his experience with this practice. He'd been feeling ill for a while, and so went to the hospital. The doctor told him that basically everything was wrong with him: he had diabetes, jaundice, problems with his heart and liver, and so forth. Further, the doctor said that because of his age, there was nothing that could be done for him. The doctor suggested that he be admitted to the hospital, where they could ensure that he'd sleep well. Essentially, he should just stay in the hospital until he died.

Because he was in a lot of pain, the doctor gave him an injection, and that was all he could do for the old man. The old man started crying because, looking forward, his life seemed so pointless. Through his tears he said to himself, "Juingong! True self! You created this body, and it's you that's causing it to hurt so much. So if I'm supposed to die, then let's get it over with! If you need me to live, then let me live. Suit yourself!"

He then left the hospital and went home. To himself, he said, "It seems like this body has become worn out and useless, so let's change it for a new one right away. Anyway, true self, take care

심하던 통증이 없어지니 밥맛도 돌아 슬슬 밥을 먹기 시작해서는 몸이 괜찮아져서 얼마 후에 다시 한번 더 병원에를 가봤답니다. 그랬더니 의사가 "어떻게 살았느냐?"고 그러더랍니다. 하하하.

 애당초에 지금 살아가는데도 '나'라고 세울 게 없는 몸뚱이인데 그냥 더불어 같이 내버리면 좋을 거를, 그 죽을까 봐 애를 쓰고 그렇게 할 필요가 뭐 있겠습니까? 아! 자기 자신의 뿌리를 진짜로 믿는 사람이라면 옷을 벗고선 바로 또 태어나도 태어날 텐데, 광대하게 태어날 텐데 말입니다. 그 헐어진 옷 한 벌이 그렇게 아까워서 그냥 벗어버리지를 못하고는 꼭 쥐고 있습니다. 그 마음으로 다 벗어버리면 얼마나 시원하겠습니까?

of this in whatever way is best." He spent several days with this attitude, when suddenly the pain vanished. This happened because his entrusting was very sincere and so was able to connect with his fundamental mind, which is connected to all the parts of his body. His intention was communicated throughout his body, where those lives began to put it into action. Because of this, his pain disappeared and he was able to start eating again. A while later, when he was feeling much better, he returned to the hospital. His doctor was amazed, asking him, "How are you still alive?!"

Inherently, we cannot say that this is "my" body, because it is actually a collection of countless different lives. So wouldn't it be nice to completely let go of the thought that it's "my" body, and just live together peacefully? Is there any need to struggle so hard to avoid death? Listen if you are someone who truly believes in your root, your foundation, then after you shed your body, not only will you take another birth right away, but you'll also be born as a great being.

지금 올망졸망한 애들을 다섯, 여섯을 놔두고도 죽어갈 때는 그 안타까운 마음 조차도 놓고 가야 되는 겁니다. 죽을 때, 깔딱 넘어갈 때, 그 순간에 모든 걸 다 놓고 가는 것처럼 그렇게 다 놓고 살라 이겁니다.

착을 두지 말고 사십시오. 착을 두지 않고도 사랑을 얼마든지 할 수 있습니다. 내 몸뚱이에 착을 안 두고도 얼마든지 살 수 있습니다. 왜 그렇게 죽을까 봐 쩔쩔 매가지고는 병원에 가서 여기 뚫고 저기 뚫고 온통 고생을 합니까? 왜 옷을 다 찢기고서야 옷을 버립니까, 글쎄. 때가 끼었든 때가 안 끼었든, 오래돼서 퇴색됐든, 그냥 퇴색된 대로 이렇게 고스란히 그냥 벗고 가면 그거 얼마나 좋습니까?

Nonetheless, people are so reluctant to take off their old clothes,[18] and instead cling desperately to those worn-out threads. If you can completely let go of all clinging to those, how relieved you'll be! Suppose you were dying right now, and were leaving behind five or six young children. You'd still have no choice. You'd have to let go of even that worry and regret, and just go. So live while letting go of absolutely everything, as if you were at the moment of death, exhaling your last breath.

Let's live without creating attachments. Love as much as you want to, but do it while not clinging to the other person. Live as good a life as you want to, but do it without clinging to your body. People become scared of dying, and so flee to a hospital where they experience terrible hardships and undergo all kinds of surgeries. Why are they so flustered with terror? Why do they have to cut their old clothes to ribbons before they can finally let go of them? No matter how old and

---

18. Clothes: In Korea, the word "clothes" is often used to describe our body. Like our body, they are something we take off at night (i.e. death), and then replace with a fresh set in the morning.

그러니까 내가 지금 얘기 한 걸 종합해서 말씀드린다면요, 이 공부를 하는 분들은 어떻게 하든지 바깥으로 끄달리지 말고 일체를 안으로 굴려 놓으시라 이겁니다. 이론적으로 다 안다고 그러지 마시고 내 근본을 굳게 믿고 모든 것을 거기에 일임해 보십시오. 내가 아무것도 모르고 묵묵히 한 발짝을 떼어 놓을 때에 그게 법이 돼야 하고, 그게 실천에 옮겨져야 됩니다. 그래야만이 우리 가정에 관한 것도, 우리 지구에 관한 것도, 이 우주에 관한 것도 모두 대처해 나갈 수 있습니다.

지난 번에 형제 법우님들이 같이 토론을 한 후 질문을 한다고 했다가 못하고 그냥 갔거든요. 오늘은 질문하실 분 있으십니까?

질문자 1(남): 안녕하십니까. 저는 충북 음성에서 태어났고, 아내는 미용일을 하고 저는 보일러 기술자로 일을 하고 있으며, 슬하에 아들 둘을 두고 있습니다. 제가 이 자리에 선 것은 폐암 말기의 선고를 받았던 환자로서의 체험담을 여러분들과 나누기 위해서입니다.

discolored your clothes are, isn't it still easier to take them off while they're intact?

My overall point is this: people who want something more out of life shouldn't allow themselves to be drawn outward by the things that happen to them. Instead, they must take everything that confronts them and return it inward. Even though you have a good intellectual understanding of what I'm saying, please, please don't mistake that for true understanding. Instead, have firm faith in your inherent foundation, and entrust every single thing there. No matter what confronts you, your practice needs to be such that when you quietly entrust something to your fundamental mind, that which you entrusted will change and manifest back into the world. Your understanding and practice have to be translated into action. Only then will you be able to truly deal with all the problems of your family, the Earth, and the Universe.

Questioner 1 (male): Hello. I came here today to share my experiences of having late-stage lung cancer. Hopefully others may find something useful in what I experienced.

지금으로부터 한 3년 전 왼쪽 가슴 아래쪽이 이상하게 아파오기 시작했습니다. 그래서, 한 내과에 가서 진료를 받았는데, 별다른 이상이 없다고 해서 일을 계속했습니다. 그런데 한 일주일이 지난 뒤에 또 다시 아파 다른 큰 병원을 찾아 검사를 받았습니다. 이 병원서는 결핵이 의심되지만, 한 달 뒤에 아무 이상이 없다고 해서, 또 일을 계속했습니다. 그렇지만 한 3개월 후 몸이 몹시 아팠고, 동네 병원에서는 폐렴에 걸렸다고 해서 2주간 입원 치료를 받고는 퇴원하여 통원 치료만 받으러 다녔습니다.

그런데 이렇게 한두 달이 지나고부터 왼쪽 가슴 아래가 너무나 아파, 큰 병원에 가서 진료를 받으니, 당장 입원을 시키더군요. 일주일간 여러 가지 검사를 다 받았고, 검사를 받는 동안 너무 초조해서 줄창 담배만 피워댔죠. 그런데 그 병원서 하는 말이 제가 암에 걸렸다는 것입니다. 처음엔 의사 선생님도 저에게 말을 못하고, 그 말을 들은 아내도 입을 떼지 못했죠. 말하라고 다그치는 저에게 아내는 그간 참았던 울음을 터뜨리며 "암이래." 하고 말했습니다.

이 말을 듣자 모든 게 거짓말 같았습니다. 마치 무서운 악몽을 꾸고 있는 것 같았습니다. 암이란 다른 사람이나 걸리는, 나와는 전혀 상관이 없는 일

About three years ago, I began to feel pain in the left side of my chest. I went to see a doctor, but he couldn't find anything wrong with me. A week later, the pain returned, so I went to a larger hospital for a full check up. They thought I might have tuberculosis, but when the results came back, everything was fine. So I just carried on with my life as usual. It was about three months after this that I became very sick and had to be hospitalized for two weeks with pneumonia.

A couple of months after that episode, I suddenly felt a terrible pain deep down in the left side of my chest. I immediately went to the emergency room and was admitted to the hospital, where I spent a week undergoing all kinds of tests. Meanwhile, I was so nervous that I was constantly smoking. When the results came back, the doctor wouldn't say anything to me, nor would my wife. When I finally got her to talk to me, she broke down into tears and choked out the words, "It's cancer."

Hearing this, it felt like my brain had been disconnected from my body, or that I was in the middle of a nightmare; nothing around me seemed real. I had never thought that cancer was

인 줄 알았는데, 제게 이런 일이 벌어지다니, 눈물 밖에는 나오지 않더군요. "저 어린 자식들은 어떻게 하나, 내 나이 이제 서른셋밖엔 안됐는데, 해야 할 일도 많고 하고 싶은 일도 너무나 많은데, 왜 내게 이런 병이 오는 걸까?" 억울하고 분하고 이루 형언할 수 없는 기분에 나오는 것이라고는 눈물밖엔 없었습니다.

그 다음날 그 병원의 과장 선생님이 우리나라에서 제일 좋은 병원의 흉부외과 교수님을 추천해 주셔서, 저는 그곳으로 가서 더 정확하고 세밀한 검사를 받았습니다. 역시 결과는 암으로 판정되었고, 수술 날짜까지 잡았습니다. 수술 전날 마지막으로 머리를 컴퓨터 촬영하게 되었는데, 갑자기 그날 저녁 수술이 보류되었습니다. 암세포가 머리까지 전이돼서 수술을 해도 소용이 없다는 것이었습니다.

이제 남은 길은 방사선 치료를 받는 것이었고, 12일간 방사선 치료를 받았는데 너무나 힘들었습니다. 머리카락도 빠지고, 몸무게도 10kg이나 빠지면서 음식을 하나도 못 먹었습니다. 담당 의사 선생님께서는 암이 머리로 전이가 된 이상, 항암제 투여를 해도 별 효과를 기대할 수 없으니, 더 이상 고통을 주지 말라고 하시면서 앞으로 3개월밖에는 못산다고 하셨습니다. 아무런 치료도 받을 수 없고 이대로

something that could affect me; it was a disease that happened to other people. I couldn't stop crying and asking, "What will happen to our two young sons? I'm only thirty-three. There are still so many things I want to do. Why is this happening to me?" Everything seemed so unfair, and I was filled with rage. No one who hasn't experienced this can understand what I felt as I sat there crying and crying.

The next day, the director of internal medicine referred us to one of the best chest surgeons in the country, so we went to see him for more detailed tests. The test results confirmed the details of the cancer, and a date for surgery was set. The day before the surgery, I had a full-body CAT scan. Suddenly, that night I was told the surgery would have to be canceled. The cancer had spread to my brain, and there was no point anymore in having the surgery.

My last chance was radiation. It lasted twelve days, and was so painful. My hair fell out, I lost ten kilograms, and I couldn't eat anything. After examining the results, my doctor wasn't hopeful. He said that with the cancer spread to the brain, we couldn't expect much benefit from chemotherapy

나가서 죽는 날만 기다려야 하다니 정말로 기가 막혔습니다. 퇴원해서 집으로 돌아 오는 동안 저와 아내는 내내 울었습니다. 집에서 애들을 봐주시던 장모님은 이제 갓 9개월이 된 저희 둘째 아들을 보면서 또 막 우시더군요. 정말 어떻게 해야 할지 모르는 절망적인 상황에서 하루하루를 보내고 있었습니다.

그런데 시골에 사시는 형님이 시골엔 공기도 좋고 하니까, 시골로 내려오라고 해서서 내려갈 준비를 하고 있는 터에, 고향에 이웃 형님 되시는 분이 전화를 하셔서 한마음선원 이야기를 해주셨습니다. 시골에 내려온 뒤 저와 집사람은 안양 본원의 큰스님을 친견하였는데, 스님께서는 "관(觀)[13]하는 것을 배우고 주인공 공부 열심히 해." 하시는 것이었습니다. 그 다음에 친견할 때에도 또 똑같은 말씀을 하셨습니다.

---

13. 관(觀): 어의적으로 '관찰하다' '보다'라는 뜻을 가지고 있으며, 마음공부를 하는 과정에서 '참나'인 주인공을 믿고 맡기는 것을 뜻함. 즉 삶에서 부딪치는 모든 문제들을 주인공만이 해결할 수 있다는 철저한 믿음으로 주인공에게 맡겨 놓고 집착 없이 지켜보는 것을 통틀어 '관'이라 함.

drugs, either. He felt that no matter what he tried, I only had about three more months to live. With so little time, and so little hope, he said there was no point in continuing such painful treatments.

Now there wasn't even the faint hope provided by these treatments. All I could do was wait to die. I was completely stunned. After leaving the hospital, my wife and I cried all the way home. My mother-in-law had come to help look after our sons, and after we told her the news, she too started crying wildly as soon as she looked at our nine-month-old son. We were so lost and hopeless, and it was so hard just to get through each day.

My older brother was living down in the countryside at our family's traditional home, and he called and suggested we come down there because the air was quite clean. As we were getting ready, one of his neighbors called me and told me about you (Kun Sunim) and Hanmaum Seon Center. So my wife and I came to see you at the Anyang main temple. You told us, "Work hard at learning how to entrust everything to Juingong, your foundation, and observe without any clinging.

처음엔 관하라는 건 뭐고, 주인공은 또 뭔가 했습니다. 그러면서도 주인공에 대해 많은 생각을 했고, 시간이 꽤 지난 어느 날 '아, 이게 바로 주인공이구나.' 하는 걸 느꼈습니다. 내 안의 근본이며 온 우주의 근본인 주인공이라는 걸 알게 되었습니다. 주인공, 그 자리에서 모든 것을 다 한다는 것을 발견하게 되었습니다. '아프게 하는 것도 주인공, 안 아프게 하는 것도 바로 주인공이구나!' 하는 것을 알게 되었고, 저는 그 주인공을 잡았습니다.

여러 차례 통증이 심해지고 했지만, 그때마다 금왕지원 주지스님께 달려가 아픔을 호소하면, "괜찮다, 주인공 자리에 맡겨라, 공부하기 전에는 나빠지느라고 아프지마는 공부하면서 아픈 것은 좋아지느라고 그러는 거니 거기다가 맡겨라." 하시는 거였습니다. 그래서 저는 흔들리는 마음을 가라앉히고 주인공한테 맡겼습니다. '네 몸이니까 네가 알아서 하라.'고요. 그렇게 하면서 편안히 마음을 놓고 있으면 어느 순간 통증이 없어지는 것을 알게 되었습니다. 죽음의 두려움이 몰려 올 때도 주인공한테 맡겼습니다.

Have firm faith in your essence, Juingong, for that is doing everything!" When we visited you again sometime later, you repeated the exact same thing.

At first I didn't know what entrusting was, nor did I understand anything about Juingong. It was only after quite some time and a lot of reflection that I began to have a feeling for what "Juingong" meant. I realized that Juingong is the foundation within me, and the foundation of the entire universe as well. As I practiced and experimented, I also discovered that this place within me called Juingong is what handles all of the things that confront me. I came to know that it is Juingong that gives rise to illness, and it is Juingong that causes illness to disappear. So I started completely entrusting everything to Juingong, and relying upon that place.

The pain got really bad several times. On those occasions, I would go visit the Hanmaum Seon Center that was near my brother's home and tell the abbot about it. He once said something that I've never forgotten: "Don't worry. Just entrust the pain to your Juingong. Before you knew anything about your foundation, you were in pain because you were becoming sicker. Now

이렇게 하기를 3년이 지났습니다. 3개월밖엔 못 산다던 제가 3년을 넘게 살고 있습니다. 주인공 공부하면서 제 스스로 맑고 긍정적으로 살려고 노력했고, 모든 것이 마음 안에서 이루어진다는 것을 알게 되었습니다. 저는 열심히 했습니다. 아프면 주인공 자리에다 맡기고 또 맡겼습니다.

저는 이제 건강이 회복되었습니다. 병원에서 진단 결과 완치되었다고 하더군요. 이 모든 게 주인공 공부하면서 이루어낸 결과라고 보아집니다. 여러분, 주인공 공부 열심히 합시다! 미쳐 봅시다. (대중 박수) 주인공은 분명히 있습니다. 끝으로 큰스님을 비롯해 여러 스님들, 제가 알고 있는 모든 분들께 감사드립니다. 정말 감사합니다.

that you understand about this foundation, the pain is arising because you are getting better. So just keep entrusting it to your foundation." I tried to set down my fear, and entrusted the pain to Juingong, thinking, "This body is yours, so what happens to it is up to you."

When I would do this and relax, there would come a moment when the pain would completely disappear. Even when I was overwhelmed with the fear of dying, I entrusted that to my foundation. I've been doing this for the last three years. The doctors told me I wouldn't last more than three months, and yet I've been able to survive for more than three years. As I've entrusted everything to this foundation, Juingong, I've worked to view everything positively, and to live with a clean and open heart. Through this, I've come to realize that everything is achieved through this inner, fundamental mind. I've really been serious about relying upon this mind. When I was in pain, I kept entrusting that to Juingong, again and again.

These days, I'm very healthy, and the doctors say that there is no sign at all of the cancer. I have no doubt that this is the result of me relying on and entrusting everything to my foundation, Juingong.

큰스님: 그럼 이제 끝났습니까? 다시 말하지만 마음 자체가 고정되어 있는 게 아닙니다. 수시로 바뀌고 수시로 바꿔서 쓸 수 있는 것이죠. 그래서 병뿐만이 아니라 모든 게 마음을 어떻게 내느냐에 따라 바뀔 수 있는 겁니다.

질문자2(남): 제가 공부하면서 체험을 통해 얻는 결과는 '내가 처리할 수 없을 정도의 일이거나 아주 봉변을 당할 수도 있는 그런 일까지도 모두 놓고 지켜보는 것이구나!'라는 것을 알게 됐습니다. 그래서 금년 여름에는 '쓰레기 통에다가 휴지를 버리듯이 아무 거리낌 없이 오는 대로 탁 놓기만 하면 되는구나!'라는 것을 느끼게 됐습니다. 그런데 그렇게 맡겨 놓고 일이 잘 해결되면 아주 개운한 맛이 있는데, 아직 일이 해결되지 않고 진행되는 과정에서는 어쩐지 그 개운한 맛이 없습니다. 그게 제가 아직 믿음이 부족해선지 아니면 그 과정에서는 다 그런 건지 그것이 좀 궁금합니다.

I'd like to say to everyone here: Be relentless in relying upon your foundation! Let's be crazy about our fundamental root, Juingong! Without a doubt, Juingong is there, underlying everything. I would like to also express my endless gratitude to Kun Sunim, the other sunims, and all the many people who have helped me and my family. Thank you very much.

Kun Sunim: Like I said before, we can change everything, not just disease, because the essence of our mind is ceaselessly changing and manifesting according to the thoughts we give rise to.

Questioner 2 (male): From my own experiences with practicing, I have come to know that we have to let go and entrust everything to this fundamental mind, including even overwhelming or humiliating things. This summer, it felt like I was able to let go of everything without having to think twice about it. It felt like simply tossing something into a wastebasket. However, one thing that I've noticed is that when I've entrusted something and it has gone well, there is a clean and clear feeling about it. But, when things haven't yet

큰스님: 회사에서도 믿는 직원한테 어떤 일을 탁 맡기면은 더 이상 신경을 안 쓰죠? 그런데 신임이 덜 가는 사람한테, 아리송한 사람한테 일을 맡겼을 때는 신경이 자꾸 쓰이는 겁니다. 하하! 그거와 똑같죠. 그러니까, 자기 근본을 완전히, 완벽하게 믿지 못했기 때문에 그런 현상이 나오는 겁니다. 완전히 믿는다면 하늘이 무너져서 내린다 하더라도 죽고 사는 것에 걱정이 하나도 없습니다. 진짜로 믿는다면 말이에요. 그렇게 '진짜 믿는다.'라는 말에는 말로는 표현 못하는 힘이 있습니다. 자리를 잡고 흐르는 물은, 고요하고 유유히 흘러도 그 흐름 안에 힘이 있는 겁니다.

이처럼 믿음이 진짜로 자리를 잡았다면 조금 이따가 죽는다 이러더라도 겁이 안 납니다. 하나도 겁이 안 나요. 모든 건 주인이 알아서 하는 거고, 난 심부름꾼이니 심부름만 부지런히 하면 되지 않겠습니까? 그렇죠?

been resolved, I notice this feeling is missing. I'm wondering if it's because my faith is a bit weak, or is that just the way things work? Is this feeling missing because the process just isn't finished yet?

Kun Sunim: When a company hands a task to a trusted employee, they forget about the problem and move on, don't they? However, when they have to give a task to someone who is less experienced or trustworthy, then they have to continually keep checking up on that person. This very same thing applies to what you're asking about. It's a sign that you aren't thoroughly and completely believing in your foundation. If you completely believe in your foundation, then even if the sky falls, you're not worried. Even life and death issues don't bother you because you know that your inherent Buddha-essence will take care of things for the best. The words "completely believe in your foundation" hint at a power that words can't contain. There is a deep power in water as it finds its place, although its flowing is calm and serene.

Like this, when your faith has become deeply rooted in your foundation, even dying won't scare you. The prospect of death won't frighten you a bit. This is because you know that this inner master

질문자 2: 제가 생활 중에 여러 일을 만나게 되는데 그때마다 제가 관하지 않은 상태에서 말을 하거나 행동을 하는 것은 다 업이 된다고 볼 수 있는지요?

큰스님: (손을 좌우로 흔들어 보이시며) 이게 자리가 잡히면요, TV를 보면서도 그냥 전체 일을 할 수 있고요, 다른 일을 하면서도 이 일을 할 수 있습니다. 그렇게 자기 근본자리를 진짜로 믿는데, 따로 관하고 말고가 어디 있겠습니까? 근본자리에서 하는 걸 아는데, 왜 그 자리에서만이 할 수 있다고 관을 따로 합니까? 진짜로 믿는데 이거 이거 하라, 이거 당신만이 해줄 수 있다 이러고 합니까? 그러니까 그렇게 하는 거는 아직 초보자가 자기 근본에 대한 믿음이 완전히 자리를 잡지 못했기 때문입니다. 그냥 이렇게 물끄러미 앉아서도 (가슴을 짚어 보이시며) 그 자리는 아주 힘이 있게 움직이며 돌아갑니다.

is what is taking care of everything that confronts you, and that your ordinary consciousness and body are just errand boys for this Buddha within us.

Questioner 2: When I react to the things in my life without first specifically trying to entrust them to my foundation, do those thoughts, words, and actions become my karma?

Kun Sunim: [shaking her head from side to side] If your practice of relying upon your fundamental mind is very settled, you can take care of everything even while watching TV. You can handle things in the unseen realm while doing other things in the material realm. When you truly believe in your fundamental mind, entrusting and observing isn't a separate, intentional thing. If you're already aware that everything is being done by this root, why should you need to separately entrust things? When you're completely aware that your foundation is doing everything, you already naturally entrust everything as soon as it comes up. When someone needs to repeatedly keep saying, "True self, only you can do this. You take care of it," they're still at the beginning level,

만약 내 근본에 대한 감사함이 절로 나온다면 나오는 대로, 안 나오면 안 나오는 대로 그대로 하십시오. '아이, 주인공 참 감사해! 살아나가는 거 모두 이렇게 돌봐줘서 감사해. 이 모든 교훈과 법을 내 스스로 나에게 이렇게 가르쳐주고 모든 일에 대처하게 해주니 참 감사해!' 이러고 자연스레 나오면 그냥 그렇게 하시라는 겁니다. 그게 진짜지요. 관하지 말란다고 스스로 나오는 것도 하지 마라 이러는 게 아닙니다.

질문자 2: 감사합니다.

and their trust in their fundamental mind hasn't completely settled down.

Even though it sometimes looks like I'm just sitting around not doing anything, this fundamental mind [placing her hand on her chest] is moving and working very powerfully. Just go forward naturally from the place of your foundation. As you do things, sometimes you'll feel grateful. so, feel grateful and go forward naturally. If you don't feel grateful, that's not a problem; just go forward naturally. When you feel grateful, go ahead and express that. For example, "Ah, Juingong, thank you so much! Thank you for taking care of everything in my life. Thank you for all the lessons and the Dharma you've taught me." When something arises naturally like that, it's very authentic, very real. When I say, "don't get too caught up in trying to intentionally or forcefully entrust and let go," this doesn't mean to suppress something when it's spontaneously arising.

Questioner 2: Thank you.

큰스님: 아까 저 분이 병을 앓으면서 그동안 지내온 이야기를 쭉 하셨는데 '그런 말은 필요 없다. 법문이나 얼른 듣고 공부해야지.' 이러지 마십시오. 남이 체험한 걸 듣는 것도 다 공부입니다. 저 분 말씀 중에 한 구절이라도 내가 지니고 의지할 수 있는 게 있다면, 그래서 발심이 됐다면 그것도 공부입니다. 이런 게 진짜 공부고 길잡이입니다.

질문자 3(남): 큰스님, 오늘 진짜로 인사 올리겠습니다.

큰스님: 하하하, 언제는 가짜구요?

질문자 3: 지난 번에는 제가 참 철이 없었습니다. 오늘 온 거는 다름이 아니라, 얼마 안 있으면 퇴직도 해야 되고 그래서 겸사겸사 한번 오고 싶었습니다. 그런데 어쩨 혼자 얘기를 하다 보니 오늘 선원에 가서 스님하고 친견을 하게 되면 모든 싹이 틀 거라고 속에서 그러더라고요. 그럴 수 있습니까? (대중 웃음)

Kun Sunim: The previous questioner spoke for quite a while about his experiences and his suffering, but even though people may talk for a long time, please don't think "Enough, already! Let's get on with the Dharma talk!" Listening to other people's experiences is also part of your practice. You may find a phrase or word that really touches your heart and helps your practice go forward. It's all practice, and it all can be a guide that shows you the way.

Questioner 3 (male): Kun Sunim! Today I am truly greeting you!

Kun Sunim: [laughs] So, the other times you were faking?

Questioner 3: The last time I was so clueless! Anyway, I really wanted to see you today. Also, I wanted to let you know that I'll be retiring soon.

I had an interesting experience as well. I've been practicing asking and speaking to my inner nature, and from inside I heard, "If you go to the Seon Center and see Kun Sunim today, the sprout will break through." Could that really happen? [audience laughs.]

큰스님: 계속 얘기 하세요.

질문자 3: 네. 그렇게 나랑 계속 얘기 하다 보니 제 속에서 제가 배우게 되더라구요. 신기했습니다. 처음에 선원에 인연된 것부터 거슬러 생각을 해 보니까 신기하더라고요.

실제로 전 선원이 있는지도, 이 도리가 뭔지도 아무 것도 몰랐습니다. 어느 날 큰스님께서 울산 KBS 공개홀에서 법문을 하셨는데, 그때 우연히 38회, 39회, 40회 회보 3장을 얻게 되었습니다. 그걸 울산 지원이 생기기 전까지 한 6개월을 주머니에 넣고 다니면서 읽었습니다. 3개월 정도밖에 안된 줄 알았는데 그게 6개월이나 됐더라고요. 그렇게 6개월을 읽으면서 '아, 나도 이 공부를 해야 되겠구나. 나하고 연관 있는 사람은 다 잘되게끔 해야겠구나.' 이런 마음을 그때 굳혔습니다. 사실 전 뭐 질문이 없습니다. 질문이 아니고 어제 내 자신과 이야기하다 보니 그런 일이 있었다는 겁니다. 단지 그 '싹이 튼다' 하는데 그게 무슨 뜻인지 잘 모르겠습니다. 그게 그냥 뭐 그런 게 있지 않나 싶으네요.

Kun Sunim: Go on, I'm listening.

Questioner 3: After I started talking with myself like that, I started learning from within myself. It's amazing!

Actually, how I first came to the Seon Center amazes me as well. I'd never heard of the Seon Center or the principle of one mind. However, one day I heard about your talk at the KBS Hall in Ulsan City, and decided to go. Right after the talk, I happened to pick up three different issues of the old Hanmaum Bulletin. I kept them in my pocket, and for months I read them over and over again. I'd been reading and thinking about what they were saying for about six months, when a Hanmaum Seon Center opened in Ulsan. All of this really instilled the feeling that I needed to practice and awaken to this fundamental mind, as well as the feeling that, through this foundation, I needed to do a better job of taking care of the people in my life. I don't have a particular question today, but I am curious about what "the sprout will break through" means. I can only guess it means that something good will happen.

큰스님: 부처님께서 하신 이야기 중에 이런 게 있습니다. 어느 집에 불이 붙었는데 아이가 아무 것도 모르고 그냥 그 안에서 놀고 앉았더랍니다. 아이를 구하긴 해야겠는데 놀라면 더 큰일이 생길 것 같아서 "애야! 빨리 나와. 내가 너 장난감을 사줄 테니까! 응?" 하고 불러내 살렸답니다. 아이를 살려내기 위한 방편으로써 그럴 수 있죠.

어떤 때는 여기 여러분도 뭔지도 모르고 그 무언가를 진정으로 믿고 천진난만하게 뛰어 들기도 합니다. 그럼 내 근본자리에서 너무나 간단히 '응, 알았어.' 이렇게 합니다. 그때는 그 대답한 놈이 책임을 지고 일을 할 수도 있는 겁니다. 아까 얘기한 대로 그냥 그대로죠. 그거를 계기로 삼아서, 그 체험을 계기 삼아 붙들고 나가라 하는 뜻입니다.

Kun Sunim: In the sutras, Shakyamuni Buddha gives the example of a house that's on fire. The house was burning, but the children were playing inside, with no idea of what was happening. Their father was outside and wanted to save them, but he was afraid that if he yelled "fire," they would panic and run further into the house. So he called out to his children, "Children, come here. Let's go and buy you some wonderful toys!" Of course, the children came running, and were saved. Although this can be described as an example of skillful means, used to encourage the children to come outside, it was also something that spontaneously arouse from his foundation.

Likewise, when you have deep faith in your foundation and just jump directly into what's confronting you, even though you don't understand what's going on, your foundation responds very straightforwardly–"Okay." The one that's responding like that is the one that's responsible for getting things done; it's the one that can take care of things. In a similar sense, what you heard about the sprout is your true self reminding you it's there. Take this experience as an opportunity to deepen your faith and your spiritual practice.

질문자 3: 오늘 여기 와서 처음부터 법문을 들었습니다. 제가 하고 싶었던 일을 한 반은 한 것 같습니다. 진짜로 제가 속이 시원합니다.

큰스님: 그렇죠. 그럼요. (웃음)
여러분은 자기 뿌리가 위대하다는 걸 아주 절실히 알아야 합니다. 자기 뿌리가 위대하다는 거, 자기 뿌리만이 자기를 리드해나갈 수 있다는 거, 그거를 명심하시고 잊지 마세요. 예수님이 이랬답디다. 나를 믿지 않고 남을 믿는다면은, 그거는 마구니 소굴이요, 그거는 도깨비 장난이라 했답니다. 각자 자기 자신을 믿으라는 소린데 고만 예수님이 자기를 믿으라는 줄 알고 내내 잘못 알고들 있지만 말입니다.

내가 생각하기엔 이렇습니다. 예수님 법도 부처님 법이요, 부처님 법도 부처님 법이요, 여러분 법도 부처님 법입니다. 세상 전부 돌아가는, 그 진리는 하나입니다. 깨달은 사람이 만 명, 십만 명이 된다 하더라도, 이 우주 간에 꽉 찼다 하더라도 진리는 하나 입니다. 하나로 돌아가는 겁니다.

Questioner 3: As I've listened to your Dharma talk today, about half the things I wanted to ask were answered or suddenly resolved. Thank you, I feel so relieved!

Kun Sunim: Wonderful!

It is most urgent that you know for yourself just how wonderful your own root is. Your root is so great, and is the only thing that can truly lead you. Never forget this! Jesus once said that those who don't believe in "me," and instead believe in others, would fall into a pit of demons or become a plaything for goblins. He was saying that we have to believe in the divine essence within each of us, but this was mistaken for believing in Jesus himself.

Here's what I think: the truth Jesus realized is the same as the truth the Buddha realized, which is the same truth that you all are living in the middle of. The truth through which the entire world functions exists everywhere and applies to all of us. Regardless of whether ten thousand people or ten million people awaken, they all realize the same truth. It is this truth through which every single thing in the universe functions

그런데 이렇게 다 함께 하나로 돌아가지만 이것조차도 고정됨이 없으니, 이렇게 하나로 돌아가는 이치도 공(空)하다고 하는 겁니다. 그저 찰나찰나 화(化)하여 나투면서 돌아갈 뿐이니 이것 또한 정해진 그 무엇이 있는 게 아닙니다. 이것이 이치이니 오고 가면서, 또, 보고 듣고 하면서 겪게 되는 모든 것을 맡긴다는 생각 없이 맡기세요. 진짜로 내 뿌리를 믿는다면 자기 뿌리를 알게 될 겁니다. 그렇게 하면서 열심히 해보세요.

옛날에 공부할 때, 물 내려가는 걸 하루 종일 봐도 그 물이 말이 없어서, 말할 때를 3일 동안이나 기다렸답니다. 내가 그렇게 미련스러웠어요. 그런데 이 공부할 때는 그런 미련함도 때론 필요합니다. 모두 열심히 하십시오. 오늘만 살고 그만두는 것 같으면 이런 소리도 아마 안 할 겁니다. 그런데 세세생생이니깐요. 그 어쩝니까?

Yet although everything functions together as one, even in this, there is nothing fixed or unchanging. This means that even the truth that everything functions together as one is empty. It continuously flows, changes, and manifests anew; there is nothing about it that you can grab onto or label. This is also how everything and everyone functions. So entrust everything you do to your foundation; entrust everything you experience, everything you see and hear. Entrust all of this while letting go of any thoughts of entrusting. If you can truly believe in your root like this, you will certainly come to know your root. Practice like this, and be diligent about it!

A long time ago, I watched a stream flowing for the entire day. The stream didn't say anything to me, so I waited and watched for three days more. It's hard to believe how stupid I was back then! That said, sometimes you need such stupidity when you want to discover and learn to rely upon your fundamental mind. Please, everyone, really try to practice hard. If we lived for only this one lifetime, I probably wouldn't tell you any of this. However, we repeatedly go through life after life. So we have to practice! This world is the middle

여기는 중세계입니다. 이제 상세계로 벗어나야 되겠죠. 상세계가 아닌 상세계로 말입니다. 그럼, 오늘은 이걸로써 끝마치겠습니다.

realm; its purpose is to sift out beings and send them on to higher or lower realms. Now is the time for us to be diligent and leave this realm for the upper realm — the upper realm that transcends all labels such as "upper realm."

Thank you all for coming. Let's stop here for today.

한마음선원본원

경기도 안양시 만안구 석수동 101-62
Tel : 82-31-470-3100   Fax : 82-31-470-3116
홈페이지 : http://www.hanmaum.org
이메일 : onemind@hanmaum.org

국내지원

강릉지원 (우)210-940 강원도 강릉시 포남2동 1304
　　　　　TEL:(033) 651-3003   FAX:(033) 652-0281

공주지원 (우)314-870 충청남도 공주시 사곡면 신영3리 152-3
　　　　　TEL:(041) 852-9100   FAX:(041) 852-9105

광명선원 (우)369-900 충청북도 음성군 금왕읍 무극4구 산5-2
　　　　　TEL:(043) 877-5000   FAX:(043) 877-2900

광주지원 (우)502-270 광주광역시 서구 치평동 201-5
　　　　　TEL:(062) 373-8801   FAX:(062) 373-0174

대구지원 (우)706-838 대구광역시 수성구 중동 532-274
　　　　　TEL:(053) 767-3100   FAX:(053) 765-1600

목포지원 (우)530-490 전라남도 목포시 상동 952-19
　　　　　TEL:(061) 284-1771   FAX:(061) 284-1770

문경지원 (우)745-823 경상북도 문경시 산양면 반곡리 449번지
　　　　　TEL:(054) 555-8871   FAX:(054) 556-1989

부산지원 (우)606-080 부산광역시 영도구 동삼동 522-1
　　　　　TEL:(051) 403-7077   FAX:(051) 403-1077

울산지원 (우)683-500 울산광역시 북구 천곡동 927-7
　　　　　TEL:(052) 295-2335   FAX:(052) 295-2336

제주지원 (우)690-140 제주도 제주시 영평동 1500
TEL:(064) 727-3100 FAX:(064) 727-0302

중부경남 (우)621-802 경상남도 김해시 진영읍 방동리 321-1
TEL:(055) 345-9900 FAX:(055) 346-2179

진주지원 (우)660-941 경상남도 진주시 미천면 오방리 50
TEL:(055) 746-8163 FAX:(055) 746-7825

청주지원 (우)360-814 충청북도 청주시 상당구 우암동 295-7
TEL:(043) 259-5599 FAX:(043) 255-5599

통영지원 (우)650-110 경상남도 통영시 도천동 113-3
TEL:(055) 643-0643 FAX:(055) 643-0642

포항지원 (우)791-220 경상북도 포항시 북구 우현동 13-1
TEL:(054) 232-3163 FAX:(054) 241-3503

Anyang Headquarters of Hanmaum Seonwon
(430-040) 101-62 Seoksu-dong, Manan-gu, Anyang-si
Gyeonggi-do, Republic of Korea
Tel: (82-31) 470-3175 / Fax: (82-31) 471-6928
www.hanmaum.org/eng
onemind@hanmaum.org

Overseas Branches of Hanmaum Seonwon
ARGENTINA
Buenos Aires
Miró 1575, CABA, C1406CVE, Rep. Argentina
Tel: (54-11) 4921-9286 / Fax: (54-11) 4921-9286
www.hanmaum.org.ar

Tucumán
Av. Aconquija 5250, El Corte, Yerba Buena,
Tucumán, T4107CHN, Rep. Argentina
Tel: (54-381) 425-1400
www.hanmaumtuc.org

BRASIL
Sao Paulo
R. Newton Prado 540, Bom Retiro
Sao Paulo, C.P 01127-000, Brasil
Tel: (55-11) 3337-5291
www.hanmaumbr.org

CANADA
Toronto
20 Mobile Dr., North York, Ontario M4A 1H9, Canada
Tel: (1-416) 750-7943 / Fax: (1-416) 981-7815
www.hanmaumcanada.org

GERMANY
Kaarst
Broicherdorf Str. 102, 41564 Kaarst, Germany
Tel: (49-2131) 969551 / Fax: (49-2131) 969552
www.hanmaum-zen.de

THAILAND
Bangkok
86-1 soi 4 Ekkamai Sukhumvit 63
Bangkok, Thailand
Tel: 070-8258-2391 / (66-2) 391-0091
home.hanmaum.org/bangkok

USA
Chicago
7852 N. Lincoln Ave., Skokie, IL 60077, USA
Tel: (1-847) 674-0811
www.buddhapia.com/hmu/chi/

Los Angeles
1905 S. Victoria Ave., L.A., CA 90016, USA
Tel: (1-323) 766-1316
home.hanmaum.org/la

New York
144-39, 32 Ave , Flushing, NY 11354, USA
Tel: (1-718) 460-2019, 070-7883-5239 / Fax: (1-718) 939-3974
www.juingong.org

Washington D.C.
7807 Trammel Rd., Annandale, VA 22003, USA
Tel: (1-703) 560-5166 / Fax: (1-703) 560-5566
http://home.hanmaum.org/wa

한마음출판사의 마음을 밝혀주는 도서

- 만가지 꽃이 피고 만가지 열매 익어
  : 대행큰스님의 뜻으로 푼 천수경 (한글/영어)
  [*2010 iF Communication Design Award* 수상]
- Wake Up And Laugh (영어)
- No River To Cross, No Raft To Find (영어)
- It's Hard To Say (영어) (절판)
- My Heart Is A Golden Buddha (영어)
- Touching The Earth (영어) (2014 출판예정)
- The Moon In A Thousand Rivers (한글/영어) (2014 출판예정)
- 생활 속의 참선수행 (시리즈) (한글/영어)
  1. 죽어야 나를 보리라
     (To Discover Your True Self, "I" Must Die)
  2. 함이 없이 하는 도리
     (Walking Without A Trace)
  3. 맡겨놓고 지켜봐라
     (Let Go And Observe)
  4. 마음은 보이지 않는 행복의 창고
     (Mind, Treasure House Of Happiness)
  5. 일체를 용광로에 넣어라
     (The Furnace Within Yourself)
  6. 온 우주를 살리는 마음의 불씨
     (The Spark That Can Save The Universe)
  7. 한마음의 위력
     (The Infinite Power Of One Mind, 2014 출판예정)
  8. 일체를 움직이는 그 자리
     (In The Heart Of A Moment, 2014 출판예정)
  9. 한마음 한 뜻이 되어
     (One With The Universe, 2014 출판예정)
  10. 지구보존
      (Protecting The Earth, 2014 출판예정)

- 내 마음은 금부처 (한글)
- 건널 강이 어디 있으랴 (한글)
- El Camino Interior (스페인어)
- Vida De La Maestra Seon Daehaeng (스페인어)
- Enseñanzas De La Maestra Daehaeng (스페인어)
- Práctica Del Seon En La Vida Diaria (Colección) (스페인어/영어)
    1. Una Semilla Inherente Alimenta El Universo (The Spark That Can Save The Universe)
- Si Te Lo Propones, No Hay Imposibles (스페인어)
- Wo Immer Du Bist, Ist Buddha (독일어)
- 人生不是苦海 (번체자 중국어)
- 无河可渡 (간체자 중국어) (2014 출판예정)
- 我心是金佛 (간체자 중국어) (2014 출판예정)

외국출판사에서 출판된 한마음도서

- No River To Cross (*No River To Cross, No Raft To Find* 영어판)
  Wisdom Publications, 미국

- Wie Fließendes Wasser (*My Heart Is A Golden Buddha* 독일어판)
  Goldmann Arkana-Random House, 독일

- Ningún Río Que Cruzar (*No River To Cross* 스페인어판)
  Kailas Editorial, S.L., 스페인

- Umarmt Von Mitgefühl ('만가지 꽃이 피고 만가지 열매 익어'
  :대행큰스님의 뜻으로 푼 천수경 독일어판)
  Diederichs-Random House, 독일

- 我心是金佛 (*My Heart Is A Golden Buddha* 번체자 중국어판)
  橡樹林文化出版, 대만

- Vertraue Und Lass Alles Los (*No River To Cross* 독일어판)
  Goldmann Arkana-Random House, 독일

- Wache Auf Und Lache (Wake Up And Laugh 독일어판)
  Theseus, 독일

- Дзэн И Просветление (No River To Cross 러시아어판)
  Amrita-Rus, 러시아

- Sub Cacing Tanah (My Heart Is A Golden Buddha 인도네시아어판)
  PT Gramedia, 인도네시아

- Wake Up And Laugh (2014년 출판예정)
  Wisdom Publications, 미국

- *No River To Cross* (*No River To Cross* 아랍어판, 제목미상)
  Sphinx Publishing, 이집트 (2014 출판예정)

- *My Heart Is A Golden Buddha*
  (*My Heart Is A Golden Buddha* 리투아니아어판, 제목미상)
  Baltos Lankos, 리투아니아 (2014 출판예정)

Books by Hanmaum Publications

- A Thousand Hands of Compassion (bilingual, Korean/English)
  [received **2010 iF communication design Award**]
- Wake Up And Laugh (English)
- No River To Cross, No Raft To Find (English)
- My Heart Is A Golden Buddha (English)
- Touching The Earth (English) (Forthcoming 2014)
- The Moon In A Thousand Rivers
  (bilingual, Korean/English) (Forthcoming 2014)
- *Practice in Daily Life* (Series) (bilingual, Korean/English)
  1. To Discover Your True Self, "I" Must Die
  2. Walking Without A Trace
  3. Let Go And Observe
  4. Mind, Treasure House Of Happiness
  5. The Furnace Within Yourself
  6. The Spark That Can Save The Universe
  7. The Infinite Power Of One Mind (Forthcoming 2014)
  8. In The Heart Of A Moment (Forthcoming 2014)
  9. One With The Universe (Forthcoming 2014)
  10. Protecting The Earth (Forthcoming 2014)
- 건널 강이 어디 있으랴 (Korean)
- 내 마음은 금부처 (Korean)
- El Camino Interior (Spanish)
- Vida De La Maestra Seon Daehaeng (Spanish)
- Enseñanzas De La Maestra Daehaeng (Spanish)

- Práctica Del Seon En La Vida Diaria (Series) (bilingual, Spanish/English)
  1. Una Semilla Inherente Alimenta El Universo
- Si Te Lo Propones, No Hay Imposibles (Spanish)
- Wo Immer Du Bist, Ist Budha (German)
- 人生不是苦海 (Traditional Chinese)
- 无河可渡 (Simplified Chinese) (Forthcoming 2014)
- 我心是金佛 (Simplified Chinese) (Forthcoming 2014)

Books available through other Publishers

- No River To Cross
  Wisdom Publications, U.S.A.

- Wake Up And Laugh
  Wisdom Publications, U.S.A. (Forthcoming 2014)

- Wie Fließendes Wasser
  German edition of *My Heart Is A Golden Buddha*
  Goldmann Arkana-Random House, Germany

- Vertraue Und Lass Alles Los
  German edition of *No River To Cross*
  Goldmann Arkana-Random House, Germany

- Umarmt Von Mitgefühl
  German edition of *A Thousand Hands Of Compassion*
  Diederichs-Random House, Germany

- Wache Auf Und Lache
  German edition of *Wake Up And Laugh*
  Theseus, Germany

- Ningún Río Que Cruzar
  Spanish edition of *No River To Cross*
  Kailas Editorial, S.L., Spain

- 我心是金佛
  Traditional Chinese edition of *My Heart Is A Golden Buddha*
  Oak Tree Publishing Co., Taiwan

- Дзэн И Просветление
  Russian edition of *No River To Cross*
  Amrita-Rus, Russia

- Sup Cacing Tanah
  Indonesian edition of *My Heart Is A Golden Buddha*
  PT Gramedia, Indonesia

- *No River To Cross* (*title to be determined*)
  Arabic edition of *No River To Cross*
  Sphinx Publishing, Egypt (Forthcoming 2014)

- *My Heart Is A Golden Buddha* (*title to be determined*)
  Lithuania edition of *My Heart Is A Golden Buddha*
  Baltos Lankos, Lithuania (Forthcoming 2014)

책에 관한 문의나 주문을 하실 분들은
아래의 연락처로 알려주십시오.

한마음국제문화원/한마음출판사

경기도 안양시 만안구 석수동 101-60
전화: (82-31) 470-3175
팩스: (82-31) 471-6928
e-mail: <u>onemind@hanmaum.org</u>

If you would like more information about these books or
would like to order copies of them,
please call or write to:

**Hanmaum International Culture Institute
Hanmaum Publications**

101-60, Seoksu-dong, Manan-gu, Anyang-si
Gyeonggi-do, 430-040, Republic of Korea
Tel: (82-31) 470-3175
Fax: (82-31) 471-6928
e-mail: <u>onemind@hanmaum.org</u>